The Experts' Guide to Life at Home

CREATED BY

S A M A N T H A   E T T U S

CLARKSON POTTER /PUBLISHERS

NEW YORK

All rights reserved.
Published in the United States by Clarkson Potter/Publishers,
an imprint of the Crown Publishing Group, a division
of Random House, Inc., New York.
www.crownpublishing.com
www.clarksonpotter.com

Clarkson N. Potter is a trademark and Potter and colophon
are registered trademarks of Random House, Inc.

This title may be purchased for business or promotional use or for
special sales. For information, please write to Special Markets
Department, Random House, Inc., 1745 Broadway, MD 6-3,
New York, NY 10019 or e-mail specialmarkets@randomhouse.com.

Library of Congress Cataloging-in-Publication Data

Ettus, Samantha.
The experts' guide to life at home / created by Samantha Ettus.
Includes index.
1. Home economics.   2. Life skills.   I. Title.
TX147.E86 2005
640—dc22   2005015391

ISBN 0-307-23756-7

Printed in the United States of America

Design by Maggie Hinders

10 9 8 7 6 5 4 3 2 1

First Edition

CONTENTS

✳

TO PROTECT

✳

✳

TO IMPROVE

✳

❋

TO BEAUTIFY

❋

✳

TO ENJOY

✳

INTRODUCTION

SAMANTHA ETTUS

I will probably never feel like I am skilled enough to create a beautiful home all by myself, and after hearing from many of you I have realized that I am in good company. In this day and age when we are all constantly on the go, trying our best to manage and balance our increasingly busy and cluttered lives, it seems like we can never do enough to improve our homes on the inside or the outside. But rather than close the book on domestic bliss, I have sought out to create one. Help is here in the form of the experts' perspective. *The Experts' Guide to Life at Home* was created to help you enjoy your home life better. It is the first book not only to offer advice on how to make your home more beautiful but also on how to live beautifully within it.

As with the first book, *The Experts' Guide to Life at Home* brings one hundred leading experts to your fingertips. Each expert lends his or her own blend of passion and wisdom to their pages, and you will see that their unique personalities and experience shine through in their chapters. I credit some contributors from the first *Experts' Guide* with whetting my appetite for more home content: I can now hang a picture on my own thanks to Barbara K; Bob Vila offered dependable painting techniques; and etiquette authority Peggy Post showed me the proper way to set a formal table. But my readers and I craved even more tips for the home, and I quickly discovered that there are volumes to be said and everyone could use some condensing.

We tend to think of our ideal home as our nest, where we live happily, dream safely, entertain, relax, express emotion, work on projects, and are most comfortable. For some of us, our home is a place where our work never ends, where as soon as one project is completed, another one erupts. Yet, for others, it is a sanctuary—a peaceful escape. In keeping with the varied intentions, luxuries, and necessities of our homes, the topics fell into six main categories of action:

- To NEST, from creating a vegetable garden to having patience
- To PROTECT, from caring for your clothing to protecting your kids online
- To IMPROVE, from controlling clutter to fixing a leaky faucet
- To BEAUTIFY, from decorating a bedroom to cleaning jewelry
- To RELATE, from balancing work and home to keeping in touch with friends
- To ENJOY, from carving a pumpkin to making holiday cookies

To create *The Experts' Guide to Life at Home,* I used my trusty technique of identifying, cold calling, and persuading the world's leading authorities on the home to share their wisdom through short chapters in their areas of expertise. For the best way to organize our closets, I sought advice from the CEO of California Closets; for the best way to impress relatives over Thanksgiving, Oprah's chef, Art Smith, weighed in on how to elegantly carve a turkey; and for mastering the art of compromise, radio psychologist, Dr. Joy Browne, shows us the way.

Just reading their advice has made me feel more domestic. I now know how to clean my pet as well as my gutters, to sharpen my knives as well as my poker skills, and I even learned how to be forgiving in the most difficult situations. Along the way, I became interested in new hobbies. Collecting authority Harry Rinker talked me into starting a collection, and scrapbooking is my new pastime thanks to talk show host and avid scrapbooker Leeza Gibbons.

As always, selecting the right expert for each chapter was perhaps the most challenging part. While Al Roker was an obvious choice for creating a family barbecue, the search for the right expert on how to fold a fitted sheet was a challenging one and it finally led me to Erik Demaine, a pioneer in the field of computational origami. And the counsel goes deeper than the how-to; when playground expert, Joe Frost, shares his advice on how to hang a tire swing, he doesn't just tell you how to do it, but also shares his understanding of why swings are beneficial to our children. Similarly, Sarah Susanka's guidance on how to make a house into a home holds your hand as you capture the full potential of your home and realize the move might not be necessary after all. And if it is, there is a chapter on how to move in the most organized way possible.

The experts have given us a gift that goes beyond their advice and tips. Infused in all of their words is their passion and devotion to what they love. Whether it is Preston Bailey waxing poetic about flowers or chef Rachael Ray describing the importance of having a "food strategy" at a ball game, these experts live their own advice. The pleasure of having one hundred experts sharing their work is that we are offered a window into their wealth of knowledge as well as their distinct loves and personalities. I hope the book encourages you to discover your own passion as well as the passion in those around you.

Read the book for entertainment-cloaked advice or consult the guide when you are preparing a dinner party, making a snowman with your kids, or simply exploring the kid inside of you. If the book motivates you to do something new or better like build a tree house, meditate, or make a birthday cake from scratch, please let me know. And remember, when you hit page 174, you are not half finished but will have half more to enjoy.

TO NEST

1

INCREASE YOUR ENERGY

JON GORDON

Jon Gordon is author of Energy Addict *and* The 10 Minute
Energy Solution. *He has served as an energy coach to the PGA
Tour, The Jacksonville Jaguars, and countless corporations
and individuals. Gordon recently hosted a month long energy
segment on NBC's* Today.

On a scale of 1 to 10, with 10 representing "I'm completely
energized" and 1 indicating "It's a miracle I get out of bed,"
think about what your personal energy meter reads. Most people
are between 4 and 7. They are overworked, overtired, and over-
stressed. We are like an energy vending machine—giving all of
our energy away and not restocking it with the right power
sources. When our family, friends, and businesses need our
energy, we are often running on empty or sold out.

The great news is that energy can be acquired through simple
strategies, action steps, and power sources.

TAKE A 10-MINUTE THANK-YOU WALK

All you need is a pair of shoes and a place to walk. While you are
walking, say out loud what you are thankful for. When you are

thankful, it's physiologically impossible to be stressed. Gratitude also enhances your happiness and health, so the thank-you walk is a great way to reduce stress and increase your blood flow, happiness, and energy at the same time. Start with 10 minutes and you'll get addicted to the way it makes you feel. Eventually you'll love it so much you'll walk for 30 minutes or take three 10-minute walks a day. So long mocha lattes—hello energy walk.

EAT BREAKFAST

Mom was right. Breakfast eaters are more productive and alert at work and have more energy in the morning. Even if you are busy, you must make time for a breakfast with protein and fiber. Suggestions include eggs and fruit, oatmeal with raisins and walnuts, hummus and an apple.

BREATHE FOR ENERGY

Throughout the day focus on your breathing to reduce stress and increase calm energy. Take 5–10 energizer breaths. Inhale for 2 seconds and exhale for 4 seconds. While you are breathing, think of a feel-good mantra, such as "Great things are happening."

TAKE A B-COMPLEX VITAMIN

The B vitamins are essential for energy production and metabolism and they also help the liver clear out stress hormones that affect your sleep and energy.

EAT MORE EARLIER

Eating more calories earlier in the day will increase your energy and help you burn more calories. Eat breakfast like a king, lunch like a prince, and dinner like a college kid with a maxed-out charge card.

GET ENERGIZED WITH YOGA, QIGONG, OR TAI CHI

A daily practice of one or more of these exercises will make a huge difference in your energy and stress levels.

EAT ENERGIZING SNACKS THROUGHOUT THE DAY

Eating healthy snacks helps you maintain your blood sugar and energy levels and increases your metabolism. Try almond butter with a celery stick or a piece of fruit and a handful of almonds.

DRINK WATER

A lack of water leads to fatigue and headaches. Many of us are not drinking enough water and are drinking too much caffeine (which acts as a diuretic), so we are dehydrated without even knowing it. Sip water every few minutes throughout the day to stay hydrated and energized.

HAVE FUN AGAIN

Children laugh about 400 times a day while adults only laugh about 25 times. Start playing again and you'll have energy too. Turn on some music and dance around your home.

SPEND 10 MINUTES IN SILENCE

We live in a noisy world and tapping the energy of silence helps us recharge our batteries and reenergize our lives. Take a daily energy break.

NEUTRALIZE THE ENERGY VAMPIRES

Don't let negative people drain your energy. Focus on your positive energy and kill them with kindness. Energy vampires are no match for your positive energy.

OTHER QUICK TIPS TO INCREASE YOUR ENERGY

* Listen to your favorite song when you need a pick-me-up.
* Surround yourself with supportive people.
* Tape your late-night shows and get more sleep.
* Eat more foods that grow on trees and plants and eat less foods that are manufactured in plants.
* Don't waste your energy on gossip, energy vampires, issues of the past, negative thoughts, or things you cannot control. Instead invest your energy in the present.
* Drink green tea. It has about a quarter of the amount of caffeine as coffee, plus it's an antioxidant that helps fight cancer and prevent heart disease.
* Smile more.
* Before you go to bed complete the following statements:
  I am thankful for . . .
  Today I was a success because . . .

2

SECURE A MORTGAGE

Melissa Cohn

Melissa Cohn is the founder and CEO of the Manhattan
Mortgage Company, a leading brokerage firm with ten offices on
the East Coast. For the past nine years she has been named Top
Mortgage Originator by Mortgage Originator *magazine.*

If you are looking to buy a home or thinking about refinancing, here is how to approach it. Start by having the following information available when you shop for your loan:

* *The purchase price of the home you are buying (or current value of your home if you are refinancing):* Contact a local realtor who can give you comparable sales for your home—the value is based upon the location, the condition, and most recent sales in the neighborhood.
* *The amount you want to borrow:* Depending on the price of your new home, there are lenders that will finance up to 100 percent of the purchase—but at a higher cost. Generally, the best rates are available if you put down 20 percent of the purchase price. But don't fear: many lenders will give you a

home equity loan for another 10 percent so that you can readily finance up to 90 percent of the purchase price.

* *Your income for the past two years:* Most banks will allow you to spend up to 40 percent or more of your gross income on your housing costs (mortgage payments and taxes/insurance). If you have great credit, there are banks that will go as high as 50 percent of your gross income to cover your monthly debt expenses.

* *Your liabilities:* These include car loans/leases, credit card debt, mortgages on other properties, student loans, and alimony child support payments.

* *When you plan to close:* The typical time for closing is 60 days. It is possible to close as quickly as 30 days, but 60 is considered the safe standard.

* *Your liquid assets:* These include cash, stocks, bonds, money market funds, and hedge funds. Banks will also consider stock options and retirement assets as part of your liquid net worth. Generally, banks look for you to have sufficient liquid assets to cover the transaction and they also require you to meet a postclosing liquidity requirement. The bigger the loan amount, the more assets your bank will want to you to have.

* *Your credit rating:* Most banks rely on a report that merges three separate credit bureaus' analyses of your credit. Your score is based on three main elements: your payment history, your debt versus your available credit lines, and the length of time you have had credit.

Each of the lenders should ask you these questions. Give them precise information so that they can give you an accurate quote on a rate.

The most important component in the whole process is to find the right mortgage lender. Don't simply approach your bank for a mortgage—it may not have the most competitive rate. Instead, shop around for recommendations. Once you have gathered your list, get an apple-to-apple comparison from each of them.

They should then be prepared to tell you the following:

* The rate they can offer you
* Whether there are any points
* The closing costs
* Length of the lock-in period
* Criteria to get you locked in
* Whether you qualify for the requested loan

These are some things to look out for in the process:

* *The rate:* Rates change daily with banks and move with the bond market. If bonds yields go up, so do mortgage rates. If you can't close within the traditional 60-day lock, ask about the cost of a longer lock-in—and get it in writing from your lender.
* *Junk fees:* Banks today charge a number of fees that aren't tax deductible and can get costly. Make sure you get a complete list of closing costs from each lender and compare them. Sometimes it pays to take a slightly higher rate if the closing costs are much lower. Keep in mind that mortgage interest is tax deductible but closing costs are not.
* *Qualifying and getting approved:* If you don't give complete information or if the lenders are not accurate in qualifying you, they can come back and tell you that you don't qualify for the rate you applied for (or were offered) but they will offer you a higher rate instead. Avoid this by getting preapproved for your financing before locking in.

MORE TIPS

PREAPPROVAL

Getting preapproved is a smart way to start the mortgage approval process in a volatile market. It should be free of charge and the bank will approve the loan without doing an appraisal of the home.

MORTGAGE BROKER

Seventy percent of all borrowers use a mortgage broker to do the shopping for them. This will save you time and money.

ADJUSTABLE RATE OPTIONS

If you are not planning on being in your home for very long, look at adjustable rate options. If your intentions are long term, consider a fixed rate—it may cost a bit more up front, but in the long run it may save you.

NEGOTIATE WITH A CONTRACTOR

Lou Manfredini

Lou Manfredini is the host of The Mr. Fix-It Show *on* WGN
Radio in Chicago and Lou Manfredini's Home Improvement
Minute *which is nationally syndicated. He has written five books
on home improvement, including the bestselling* Mr. Fix-It
Introduces You to Your Home. *He is the home contributor for*
NBC 's Today, *a columnist for* USA WEEKEND *magazine,
and Ace Hardware's "Helpful Hardware Man."*

As a builder for over twenty years, I have made my share of
mistakes. However, if I had to point to one nuance that I have
learned from my experience, it is how to create contracts that are
fair to all involved and a transparency in the way we charge our
clients.

Whether you are remodeling your bathroom or kitchen, or
adding a new deck, you are likely emotionally attached to the
project. I have seen so many people make emotional decisions
when it comes to hiring a professional to work on their home. It

is important to approach your project with an aura of detachment, looking at it as a business proposition. Your contractor, while important to get along with, is doing your project to make money. The reason you hear the phrase "Get three bids" is that it's an opportunity to see where the numbers are going to fall. When all parties realize why everyone is at the dance, the better the entire experience will be.

The first step is to define the project as precisely as possible to all potential contractors. The easiest way is to have a detailed blueprint created so that every potential contractor is looking at the same scope of work before bidding. If your project is not big, you should create an outline for all to look at instead. Make sure that all of your contractors are licensed, insured, and bonded, if necessary, and that they will provide you with waivers of liens for materials and payments to subcontractors.

As for insurance, they should be covered for general liability insurance in case they damage your home as well as worker's compensation for their crew. With these initial credentials along with glowing references, you are setting the table for a well managed and fun experience. Have all the contractors bid completely on the work you want done. Make sure any contingencies that they have addressed have a dollar amount. While most projects go over budget, having a better idea of the total number will better assist you in creating a wise cash flow plan.

Once you receive the bids, go over each proposal to confirm they are all completing the work you want done. Then bring those contractors back individually to see if you can get the pricing to a sharper number. Remember that the lowest number is not always your best value. Ask each contractor about their suppliers, the materials they plan to use, and alternatives that may lower the price but not the quality of the work. Most contractors will create a template for the work to be done that includes cost for materials, their subcontractors (if it is applicable), and appropriate markups as well as a general profit margin for running the job.

One system that I recommend is a "cost-plus contract." Here is how it works: All hard costs for materials and subcontractors' profit and overhead are laid out. Then, to control your cash flow, you write checks directly to the contractor's suppliers or subcontractors on a specified payment schedule, typically monthly, depending on the length of the project. Each month you also write a check to the contractor for his or her profit and overhead. If the job gets bigger owing to changes, so does the profit and overhead to the contractor. While you will be writing more checks with this plan, you will also know precisely where your money is going. It also gives you waivers of liens to protect you from any potential lawsuits that occur if the contractor does not pay his bills.

MOVE INTO A NEW HOME

Linda Rothschild

Linda Rothschild is the founder and CEO of Cross It Off Your List, a New York–based relocation, organization, and lifestyle management consulting firm. She is a past president of the National Association of Professional Organizers.

Across the street or across the country, there's no doubt about it: moving is a traumatic experience. The average American moves twelve times during the course of his or her lifetime, and the process is said to be one of life's three most stressful events. And no matter how long you procrastinate, the time will come when everything in your home has to be moved. The key to success is to manage the process by being prepared and organized.

SORTING AND ORGANIZING

This is the time to sort through your possessions and make good decisions about what to keep. Let go of the things you no longer need and always recycle what is in good shape. There is someone out there who needs it more than you do.

KNOW WHERE EVERYTHING IS GOING

Our first instinct is to think about the furniture. What about the luggage and the sports equipment? Will you have more or less storage space than your last home? Measure, photograph, and plan ahead. Use Post-it notes to identify what rooms things are going to.

HIRE A MOVING COMPANY

Unless you have three or four really strong helpers in your life, do not attempt to move on your own. Instead, hire a mover. It is money well spent and will save not only time but your lower back! Always get a recommendation from someone who has had a good experience. Movers are generally busiest the first, the fifteenth, and the end of the month. Get a binding estimate or flat rate so that you will know what to expect. Remember that this is your life, your home, and your worldly possessions, so the cheapest way is not always the best.

PACK PROPERLY

Packing is deceiving. It always takes more time and more boxes than you think. If you are organized when you pack, unpacking will be much easier. Mark boxes with a number on all four sides and on the top write in what room it needs to be placed. Keep an inventory on paper of what is in the boxes. It will be easier to locate what you are looking for on paper than sifting through a pile of boxes.

UNPACK EFFICIENTLY

Stay organized when putting things away to keep your new home organized for good. Work room by room instead of running all over the house. Prepare a place to work and be thorough. Small items get lost easily in packing paper. Have just one or two people available to help unpack and haul empty boxes and paper. Too much help is not always a good thing, especially if they don't know where things belong.

CREATE A MOVING TIME LINE

As soon as you know you are moving, create a plan. Sit down with a large calendar on which you can write your "To Do" lists and, starting 6 weeks ahead of your estimated moving date, fill in the following:

6 WEEKS AHEAD

* Pick moving dates. This can be multiple days. Include time for packing, loading the truck, driving to the new location, and unloading.
* Gather estimates from movers. Do not accept an estimate over the phone and be clear about what is going to be moved before asking for an estimate.
* Visit the new location or get a good floor plan, including storage spaces for planning where things will go.

4 WEEKS AHEAD

* Begin sorting and organizing.
* Hire a mover.
* If you are packing yourself, get your moving supplies now.
* Send out anything that needs to be repaired or cleaned.
* Change utilities to your new home.
* Change postal address and addresses for bills. Remember that magazines take a few months to catch up with a new address.
* Collect medical records and transfer prescriptions, if necessary.

2 WEEKS AHEAD

* Complete sorting and organizing your home.
* Arrange for donations, carting, trash removal, and recycling.

* Plan meals around what you have in the freezer and pantry.
* Change newspaper delivery.

1 DAY AHEAD

* Be sure the new home is clean before moving in.
* Plan the first box. Whatever you will need immediately—toilet paper, paper towels, coffeemaker—should go in it.
* Pack a suitcase of personal items you will need for the next few days. Include toiletries, medications, and clothing.
* Pack linens and towels so everyone can sleep and shower the next day.
* Pack a box of cleaning supplies to have on hand when you arrive.
* Be clear about payment arrangements with mover and gratuities.
* Get a good night's sleep. You'll need it.

DAY OF MOVE

* Inventory furniture and boxes well to make it easy to find things.
* Bond with the movers—especially the foreman. You want this to go as smoothly as possible.
* Do a final walk-through to make sure the house is empty before the movers leave.
* Walk the movers through the new home before they start bringing anything in. Put signs on each room so movers know which room is which.
* Start unpacking rooms in order of importance. Bedrooms and bathrooms should come first.

Moving can be a smooth process instead of a stressful nightmare if you plan ahead. Use this opportunity to make your new home streamlined and uncluttered—a good foundation for any new beginning.

5

MAKE A BUDGET

LYNNETTE KHALFANI

Lynnette Khalfani is a money coach and author of the New York Times *bestseller* Zero Debt: The Ultimate Guide to Financial Freedom. *She writes a weekly newspaper column called Financially Fit and is a former reporter for* The Wall Street Journal.

Most people dread being on a budget. The word alone conjures images of deprivation, making us think about everything we can't have, can't do, or can't buy. But creating a budget—and living with it—doesn't have to be so restrictive.

Having a good budget offers a host of benefits:

* It gives you power and control over your finances.
* It keeps you from living paycheck to paycheck.
* It allows you to save for future goals and dreams.
* It helps you avoid going into debt.

Here's a simple, two-step system you can use to create a livable budget, one that will help you achieve peace of mind and eliminate worries about your money.

STEP 1: MAKE A LIST OF YOUR EXPENSES

Begin by itemizing all the areas of your life where you spend money. Some common categories are:

* Food
* Housing
* Entertainment
* Transportation
* Debts
* Utilities
* Educational costs
* Childcare
* Insurance
* Miscellaneous

When you make your list, think about how you live on a daily and monthly basis. If you have kids for whom you regularly buy gifts, include a gifts category. If you're an avid reader, enter a category for magazine subscriptions or books.

Once you have the right categories, don't make the mistake of underestimating your expenses. I've seen people budget zero money for travel or vacations and justify this omission by saying, "Well, some years I don't take *any* vacations." And don't gloss over purchases that occur only once in a while. All those trips to the vending machine at work each week can add up. By low-balling the costs of these items, you can wreck your budget. If your bank were to issue you a statement based on the amount of cash you *should* have in your account, that number would be inflated, and seeing an artificially high balance in your checking account might spur you on to spend money you don't have.

STEP 2: ADJUST TO AVOID BUDGET BUSTERS

If your expenses exceed your income, you'll have to cut back on areas that aren't necessities. Unexpected events and emergencies will always come up, but you can minimize their impact by adjusting your budget according to the principle of LIFE, an acronym that describes the four ways in which your budget can get out of whack:

* Listed items are undercalculated.
* Impulse purchases seduce you.
* Forgotten bills surface.
* Emergency or unexpected events occur.

LISTED ITEMS ARE UNDERCALCULATED

L stands for expenses that are *listed* items in your budget, but your numbers are actually off the mark. For example, if your credit card bills show that you spend $250 a month on clothes, don't put $100 into the clothing category. Additionally, make sure the figures you list in your budget for things like cell phone service or utilities are accurate even when they appear to be "fixed" costs. Add in taxes, regulatory fees, and surcharges on your cell phone bill. And allow for those months when you go over your allotted minutes. List a realistic number based on your past usage and spending patterns.

IMPULSE PURCHASES SEDUCE YOU

I refers to the *impulse* purchases that everyone makes now and again. Anytime you make an unplanned purchase—whether you're shopping online or happened to find something too good to be true while "just window shopping"—that's an impulse purchase. Keep those to a minimum.

FORGOTTEN BILLS SURFACE

F is for those *forgotten* bills that pop up when you least expect them. Some bills get paid annually or perhaps twice a year—like your gym membership or your auto insurance. To avoid this being short of cash when these bills are due, just factor them into your budget on a pro-rated basis and put the money aside. For instance, if your auto insurance is $1,200 a year and it's due in December, enter $100 a month in your budget for this expense and put that amount aside each month instead of trying to come up with all of the money at the end of the year.

EMERGENCY OR UNEXPECTED EVENTS OCCUR

E is for *emergency*. There are times when emergencies—like a burst boiler unit—can ruin a budget. Try to minimize these events with preventive measures, such as regularly servicing your boiler, having routine maintenance done on your car to avoid breakdowns, and making periodic visits to the doctor to stave off serious medical conditions.

Once you prepare for LIFE, you can take steps to safeguard your finances and create a realistic budget you can live with. And, for most of us, that's the first step in achieving financial freedom.

MAKE A HOUSE INTO HOME

SARAH SUSANKA

Sarah Susanka is an architect and author whose Not So Big *series of books and* Home by Design *have sold over a million copies. She is credited with pioneering the "build better, not bigger" movement. Her most recent book is* Inside the Not So Big House. *She is a columnist for* Inspired House *magazine.*

Many of us live in houses that are ill suited to the way we actually live. We have spaces that only get used once in a blue moon, while others get used constantly.

So what can be done to make your house fit you like a well-tailored suit rather than a "one size fits all" sack? The chances are good that the spatial resources you need are right there in your house already.

UNTAPPED RESOURCES

The first step in revealing your home's hidden spatial treasure is to find out how you are using your existing rooms and spaces.

The exercise below will allow you to identify spaces that could be "repurposed" or that could do double duty. Start by making a chart with four columns:

1. *Room name:* In the first column, make a list of all the rooms and spaces in your house.
2. *Frequency of use:* In the next column, write down approximately how many times a week the room is used. If it's all day, every day, write down "constant." If it's less than once a week, write down the approximate number of times per year instead.
3. *Square footage:* Take measurements of each room and write down the square footage of each space in the third column.
4. *Size rating:* In the final column, identify which is the largest room, next largest, and so on.

Now take a look at the results. Many people are surprised to discover that they've actually got several rooms—often the biggest ones—that are largely dormant, waiting for important, but apparently nonexistent, guests to arrive. Meanwhile, the real household members are crammed into the smaller and less desirable rooms.

The second step is to analyze what spaces are underutilized. On your chart, underline the rooms that are used less than three times a week. Of these, identify which are used less than once a month, and give them a second underline. These are your primary spatial resources, and they're just waiting for you to live into them.

If you have a formal living room, for example, that gets used only a couple of times per year, this is a prime candidate for repurposing. A foyer that's only used when solicitors come to the door is raw space that's costing you money to heat and cool and is grossly underutilized in terms of livability.

If you have a formal dining room that gets used only for Sunday dinners, you might consider making this room do double duty as something else during the other six days a week.

WISH LISTS

The third step is to make two lists, one that identifies all the functions and activities that make you feel cramped and the other that identifies functions and activities that you believe your house cannot accommodate.

Imagine the possibilities. On the first list you might include such things as:

* Can't see the television or the family when I'm preparing dinner
* Bathroom a perpetual madhouse in the morning
* Always accidentally kicking cat food bowl when I make coffee

On the second list identify such needs and desires as:

* Place where kids can paint, without worrying about mess
* Space for 10 boxes of books that we've never unpacked
* A better informal eating area with a view to yard

These two lists collectively identify the things that are keeping you from feeling completely at home in your own house.

The fourth and final step is to bring your wish lists together with your list of untapped spatial resources and to find spots for as many of the wish lists items as you can. If you go through this process creatively, you'll be surrounded with places for the activities that make household members feel both fulfilled and nurtured, and you'll have discovered the most important act in turning your house into a home—making it truly tailored to the way you live.

CREATE A HOME OFFICE

LISA KANAREK

Lisa Kanarek is the founder of Home Office Life, a firm that

advises corporations and individuals on all aspects of working

from home. She is the author of several books, including Home

Office Solutions: Creating a Space That Works for You.

Setting up a home office can be a luxury or a necessity depending on your situation. Make sure that as you put yours together, what you will be using it for stays at the top of your mind.

LOCATION

Before you decide where to set up your home office, carefully evaluate every room and ask yourself the following questions:

* Will distractions be kept to a minimum in this area?
* Is there ample lighting?
* Is there enough room for all of your equipment, files, and supplies?
* Are there enough electrical outlets?
* Would it be difficult to run a phone line and Internet access wiring into this space?

By answering these questions, you will identify the best space for a home office.

DESIGN

Keep your home office from becoming an eyesore by designing it to reflect your taste, interests, and style. Plan ahead by measuring your space before you buy any new furniture. Whether you want a simple writing desk (ideal for a notebook computer) with a lap drawer for supplies or a large desk with file drawers, determine whether the piece is functional and then decide if it matches your décor. Look for an ergonomically correct desk and chair as well as a bookcase to store books. If your space is limited or you need to "close your office doors" at the end of the day, an armoire with enough space to house your office equipment is ideal. Invest in quality furniture.

If your office isn't carpeted, add an area rug to minimize echo. For privacy and to ease the impact of direct sunlight, add window treatments. Be sure to provide enough light for your desk and overall office. If you are going to meet with clients in your office, set up a space complete with guest chairs and a meeting table.

FLOOR PLAN

Decide which of the five basic home office furniture arrangements is best for your space: L-shaped, U-shaped, parallel, corner, or reverse-corner arrangement.

* The L-shaped work area is ideal if you have limited space. It offers the advantage of getting equipment off your desk and onto a secondary surface.
* The U-shaped work area is ideal if you need to spread out papers while you work or if you need extra equipment (e.g., scanner,

copier) nearby. It allows you to keep everything within reach on three surfaces.

* The parallel layout is ideal for meeting with clients. When they walk into your home office, you will face them rather than have your back to them.

* The corner arrangement and reverse-corner arrangement are ideal if you need to make the most of a small space or an awkward corner. You'll increase your storage space by adding a hutch on the left and the right. Two-corner arrangements facing into each other with hutches on both sides are ideal for a couple sharing a home office. This arrangement includes a desk with returns on each side. The desk either faces into the corner or out into the room.

STORAGE

Ample storage space is a necessity. Be creative. Instead of using a gray metal file cabinet, find alternatives. You could store files in a wooden or wicker ottoman, below a window seat with file frames inside the drawers, or inside a decorative wooden trunk. Keep files you use often nearby by using a desk with at least two deep file drawers.

ORGANIZING

Don't rely on your memory to plan your days. Invest in some type of planning system, whether paper-based, computerized, or electronic. Set up an easy-to-use filing system using hanging folders for main categories with interior folders inside.

TECHNOLOGY

Equip your office with the best technology you can afford, including a computer that is as fast as possible and loaded with more memory than you think you'll need. Consider purchasing all-in-one equipment that faxes, prints, copies, and scans documents in color. The smaller footprint (and often low price) of these machines makes them ideal for most space-challenged home offices. A high-quality phone, a high-speed Internet connection, and a reliable backup system are crucial elements of a home office.

BOUNDARIES

Working from home offers many distractions including not only household chores but family and friends wanting to visit. Before you share a home office with your spouse, consider whether you have compatible working styles. Set certain hours for working in your home office. If you aim for a specific time to start your day, it will be easier to avoid being sidetracked on your way to work, even if your commute lasts only a few seconds.

8

ORGANIZE YOUR FINANCES

DAVE RAMSEY

Dave Ramsey is the best-selling author of The Total Money
Makeover *and* Financial Peace. *His nationally syndicated radio
program* The Dave Ramsey Show *is heard on more than
250 stations throughout the United States.*

Getting your finances organized is crucial if you are going to
win with money. People often tell me they are trying to save,
invest, or pay off debt, but they can't get any traction. Here's
what I tell them.

1. STOP WHINING AND DO SOMETHING ABOUT IT. Don't walk
   around like Gomer Pyle on Valium. Advertisers have a plan to
   make you want to buy their products, so you need to get on a
   plan and stick with it. Set some goals and get intense about
   reaching them.

2. MAKE A WRITTEN BUDGET. This is not a form of medieval tor-
   ture. It is you telling your money what to do instead of wondering where it went. You have to make your money behave
   and a written plan is the whip and chair for the money tamer.
   Set up a new budget every month. Don't try to have the perfect

budget for the perfect month because we never have those. Spend every dollar on paper before the month begins. Give every dollar of your income a name before the month begins—this is called a zero-based budget. Income minus outgo equals zero every month. Look at this month's income and this month's bills, savings, and debts, and match them up until you have given a name to every income dollar and outgo. Don't forget to budget for things that don't happen every month like car insurance and Christmas. (It's in December this year; don't let it sneak up on you.)

3. GET RID OF YOUR CREDIT CARDS. Have a plasectomy (the creative destruction of credit cards). If you play with snakes, you get bitten. Credit cards enable you to buy things you can't afford. "But I pay them off every month." CardTrak says 60 percent of you don't pay off your credit cards every month. "But I want the free airline miles." *Consumer Reports* says 75 percent of the airline miles are never redeemed.

4. USE THE ENVELOPE SYSTEM. Look at your budget and see how much you budgeted for groceries. At the beginning of the month go to the bank and take out that amount of cash; put the cash in an envelope marked "Groceries." When you go to the grocery store, use this cash to pay for them. When the envelope is empty stop spending! Do the same thing for eating out, entertainment, and clothing. When you use cash, it hurts more than when you use a credit card. If you don't like to carry a lot of cash, use a debit card. You can do everything with a debit card that you can do with a credit card except go broke.

5. SAVE FOR EMERGENCIES. It *is* going to rain. You need an umbrella. *Money* magazine says that 78 percent of us will have a major nega-

tive event in a given 10-year period of time. Life happens, so be ready. You need an old-fashioned Grandma's rainy-day fund. Sometimes people tell me I should be more positive. Well, I *am* positive: it is going to rain, so you need a rainy-day fund. If you have debt—credit cards, car payments, and so on—then you should save $1,000 for emergencies. This is enough to keep you from adding to your credit card debt for things like flat tires and doctor co-pays. If you are totally out of consumer debt, you should save 3–6 months of expenses for life's big emergencies like illness, blown engines, and layoffs.

6. GET OUT OF DEBT! You can do so much more when you have total control of your greatest wealth-building tool—your income. Imagine what you could do if you didn't have to pay MasterCard or GMAC every month. You could prepare for retirement or your child's education. You could buy that leather couch (with cash, of course) or take that vacation you've always wanted. Besides, the car drives so much better when it's paid for. List your debts from smallest to largest and attack that smallest one with a vengeance while you only pay minimums on the rest. Once the smallest is paid move on to the next smallest and so on. I call it the debt snowball because the amount of money you put toward each debt grows as you roll down your list of debts.

Once you have your finances in order I promise you'll find a peace you've never known before and you can concentrate on other things— like having fun!

9

FILE TAXES

BERT N. MITCHELL

*Bert N. Mitchell is founder and chairman of Mitchell & Titus
LLP, the nation's largest multicultural CPA and management
consulting firm. As former president of the New York State
Society of CPAs, he was the first African American to head a
professional state society in the United States. He is the author of
more than fifty published articles and has received numerous
awards, including the AICPA Gold Medal Award for
Distinguished Service, the accounting profession's
most prestigious award.*

Taxes are feared, dreaded, and—unfortunately—inevitable!
Like the holiday season, the tax preparation process is an
annual one. Every year most people kick into a regular routine to
deal with the myriad responsibilities that the holiday season
brings. The tax preparation season is no different. You can help
eliminate a lot of anxiety by not waiting until April 14 or, worse,
April 15 to begin the preparation process.

Here I have identified some simple and effective steps to assist you in preparing your individual tax return. Please keep in mind that everyone's tax situation can vary! If you have specific questions, contact your tax preparer or IRS representative.

1. DETERMINE YOUR ACTION PLAN
PRIOR TO THE END OF THE TAX YEAR

You should be thinking about the tax preparation process throughout the year, and with few exceptions tax-planning strategies must be in place by December 31 of the tax year. You may be eligible to take advantage of a variety of tax deductions, and it is a good idea to incorporate these expenses into your annual budget and keep track of them throughout the year.

Other important tax questions to consider before year's end include:

* Do I owe estimated taxes? (self-employed and 1099 taxpayers)
* Is my state and federal withholding sufficient? (W-2 employees)
* Am I entitled to retirement-planning tax benefits? (those age 65 and older)
* Have I taken advantage of college savings plan benefits?
* Have I implemented the appropriate estate planning and planned giving strategies?

2. CHOOSE YOUR METHOD

Decide if you are going to utilize a professional tax preparer, or the self-preparation method. If you decide to do it yourself, there are a wide variety of user-friendly software packages and books available. Additionally, the IRS publishes Form 1040 and the corresponding instructions, which are available at local post offices, your local IRS

Taxpayer Assistance Center, and the IRS Internet site www.irs.gov. Many taxpayers are eligible to use free online tax preparation software to e-file a paperless income tax return (www.irs.gov/efile).

If you decide to seek professional help, there are a wide variety of tax preparation services available, from local franchises to large international CPA firms. Make sure that the tax preparation service you choose is well qualified. Ask for references.

3. ESTABLISH AN ANNUAL ROUTINE
TO ORGANIZE YOUR IMPORTANT DOCUMENTS

Designate a file cabinet, folder, or desk drawer to store your important tax documents. It is helpful to use bookkeeping software to code and categorize your annual expenses. You should categorize expenses as personal, household, or business expenses. Make a checklist that you can review annually to help you keep track of records from the prior year. Most official tax documents are mailed by your employer, banks, mortgage companies, and brokerage houses between the end of January and the end of February of the succeeding tax year.

The following information and documents should be maintained in preparing your income tax returns:

* Wage information (W-2s 1099s, employment check stubs)
* Social Security benefits
* Interest or dividend income
* Estimated tax payments
* State tax refunds
* Capital gains and losses
* Mortgage interest expense information
* Records of charitable contributions
* Medical, child care, and education expenses

* Business expenses (including home office, travel, meals, and entertainment)
* Year-end credit card statements and receipts from large purchases
* Vehicle expenses

There are limits to the amount of itemized deductions that individual taxpayers can use to reduce their taxable income. Some frequently overlooked deductions include appraisal fees for charitable donations, cellular telephone expenses used for business, moving expenses, job-seeking expenses (in your present occupation), points on home mortgage, professional organization dues, state and local taxes paid, safety deposit box fees, and tax preparation fees.

Also make note of any changes in circumstances during the year that may affect your filing status (e.g., marriage, birth of child, death of a spouse, sale of a primary residence, or relocation to a new state).

4. ALLOW ADEQUATE TIME FOR THE
PREPARATION AND REVIEW OF YOUR TAX RETURN BEFORE FILING

If you are not prepared by April 15, you can file an extension (Form 4868), which grants an automatic four-month extension of time to file. This form must be filed by April 15. It is an extension of time to file, not an extension of time to pay.

Regardless of the method you choose, you will avoid unnecessary errors by allowing enough preparation time. Review your return and make a copy before filing it. When mailing your income tax return, make sure you are using the correct amount of postage, and the appropriate IRS address. Finally, do not forget to sign and date your tax return!

MEDITATE

JOEL AND MICHELLE LEVEY

Joel and Michelle Levey are cofounders of Seattle-based
InnerWork Technologies, Inc., a firm that specializes in
developing and renewing organizational cultures to focus on
harmony and balance. They have written a number of books,
including A Moment to Relax: Stress Relief in Minutes.

Meditation offers practical health benefits, such as relaxation, peace of mind, enhanced vitality, and performance, as well as the extraordinary benefits of awakening you to the sacred dimensions of life. By refining the quality of attention and intention that you bring to life, meditation can optimize virtually everything you do.

Meditation practice transforms confusion into wisdom, mindlessness into mindful presence, habitual reactivity into freedom, insensitivity into compassion, personality into essence, and isolation into a profound state of deep relationship with all creation. Within the world's diverse wisdom traditions, there are millions of highly practical methods of meditation. This orientation will guide you into the basic essentials of successful meditation practice.

THE FOUNDATION

As you reduce the turbulence in your relationships, your mind naturally becomes more peaceful, powerful, and present. The opposite is also true! "Right relations" lay the foundation for meditation to be fruitful.

MEDITATE ON PURPOSE

Be clear on your intention. Are you meditating in order to relax and ease your stress? To cultivate greater clarity or peacefulness? Or, perhaps, to increase your capacity to inspire and help others?

PHYSICAL POSTURE

* Your body should be in a balanced, comfortable position with your spine straight.
* Eyes should be closed or softly half open.
* The Buddha taught that the practice of meditation has four postures: sitting, walking, standing, and lying down. Taking this advice to heart, every activity can be transformed from mindless habit into a practice for awakening more fully.

TIME AND QUALITY

Begin with short 5-minute meditation sessions. Add time as the quality of your attention improves.

DISTRACTION AND SLEEPINESS

When your attention wanders, return your focus to your meditation. Allow thoughts to come and flow without getting involved with them. Gradually, the mind will become more clear, calm, and stable. If you are drowsy when meditating, open your eyes, do standing, walking, or moving meditation, or stop meditating and take a nap.

INTEGRATION

A meditation session ideally has three phases: setting intention, actual practice, and integration carryover. Once you conclude your formal meditation session, make a conscious intention to carry that quality of presence cultivated through your meditation into action.

MEDITATIONS

Reach out to the sources of inspiration in your life who support you in awakening to your true nature and highest potential. Inhaling, envision receiving waves of energy, inspiration, and love from them. As you exhale, open your heart-mind, radiating this inspiration and energy to your loved ones, friends, colleagues, patients, or students, and through them to all whose lives they will touch, directly or indirectly. Rest in this easy, natural flow, receiving and radiating.

FOCUSING MANTRAS

To bring clarity, calm, balance, and focus to your mind, synchronize the easy, natural flow of your breath with one of the following sets of words, which serve as mantras (mind protection from random mind chatter): "Here" (in breath), "Now" (out breath); "Focus" (in breath), "Flow" (out breath); or "Om Mani" (in breath) "Pedme Hum" (out breath).

MINDFUL PRESENCE

Mindfully rest within the flow of every changing, moment-to-moment experience. Begin by following the natural flow of your breath, adding a gentle smile to your mindful presence. (This will protect you from trying too hard or being too self-critical.) Mindfulness of this effortless natural breath flow is your resting place of awareness, the place where you come home to.

As perceptions, sensations, thoughts, or images, emotions, desires, or intentions arise, simply notice how they all come and go. Discover how everything is in flow and connected. While sitting, walking, or even talking, weave this mindful presence into every moment and circumstance of your life.

LOVING-KINDNESS MEDITATION

As a focus for your meditation, repeat the following phrases quietly to yourself:

> *May I be happy and peaceful.*
> *May I be healthy and strong.*
> *May I be filled with loving-kindness.*
> *May I fully awaken and be free!*

Expand this meditation by holding others in your heart-mind, saying, "May you . . ." and "May all beings. . . ." Go for the feeling behind the words and discover the true radiance of your heart.

11

GROW A VEGETABLE GARDEN

HOWARD GARRETT

Howard Garrett is a landscape architect and a natural

organic consultant. He is the author of more than twelve books,

including The Dirt Doctor's Guide to Organic Gardening. *His*

column, The Natural Way, appears weekly in the

Dallas Morning News.

There are three keys to growing food crops. Start by getting rid of all the toxic chemical pesticides and high-nitrogen synthetic fertilizers. Next, increase the health of the soil by adding natural organic amendments. Finally, plant indigenous and well-adapted plants and maintain them with natural organic techniques. If plants are happy where they are planted, they will grow well and have few problems.

BUILDING HEALTHY SOIL

If you choose products and techniques that are good for the life in the soil, successful gardening will come easily. Compost is the most important soil amendment. It can be made at home or pur-chased ready-to-use.

Compost piles can be started any time of the year and can be placed in sun or shade. Add leaves, hay, grass clippings, tree trimmings, food scraps, bark, sawdust, rice hulls, weeds, nut hulls, and any animal manure. Mix the ingredients together in a container or simply pile the material on the ground. Maintain the moisture of a squeezed-out sponge to help the living microorganisms thrive and work their magic. Compost is ready to use when the ingredients are dark brown, no longer identifiable, and soft and crumbly with the fragrance of the forest floor. Turn the pile once a month to speed up the process. Purchasing quality compost from the local garden center or feed store is the most practical way to start.

The following amendments should be forked or tilled into the native soil prior to planting the seeds or transplants: compost, organic fertilizer, lava sand or other volcanic sand, and whole-kernel cornmeal. Additional ingredients that are helpful include molasses, coffee grounds, and earthworm castings.

STARTING SEEDS INDOORS

All plants can be started indoors or out. The advantage to starting indoors is that gardeners get a jump on the season by setting out transplants when the weather is warm enough. Light is not needed for germination, so use the top of the refrigerator and other out-of-the-way places. The windowsill is usually a poor place to germinate seeds because the temperature can greatly fluctuate. Any potting soil will do, but my favorite is equal amounts of compost, expanded shale, and coconut fiber.

After sprouts emerge, move them to a sunny place. Prevent seedlings from leaning toward the light by turning the containers daily. Low light will cause seedlings to stretch and weaken. Water the seedlings gently and check the soil several times a day. Plants indoors can dry out quickly and may need to be watered more than once a day.

Organic fertilizer should be added to the soil after seedlings grow to about an inch tall. Earthworm castings and compost are good choices for young plants. Compost tea (tea made from soaking compost in water) at 1 cup per gallon can be used as a foliar feeding material and as excellent mild fertilizer for the soil and roots.

Introducing young plants to an outdoor environment should be done gradually on a mild day. Leave plants in partial shade and protect them from wind for a few hours the first day. Extend their exposure time each day. In 3 or 4 days, young plants should be acclimated to sunlight and be able to stay out in the full sun. Move them back indoors if the weather changes abruptly.

STARTING SEEDS OUTDOORS

Broadcast vegetable and herb seeds on the prepared soil and cover them with a thin layer of earthworm castings or finely screened compost. Water them gently and keep soil moist until the small seedlings are growing. Sprinkle cornmeal on the beds to prevent diseases. Drench and/or spray garlic tea to prevent insect pests. Add a thin layer of compost as mulch.

TRANSPLANTING SEEDLINGS

Flats or pots of plants always need to have a good soaking before planting. Soak the plant roots in a bucket of water with compost tea until they are saturated. They should be sopping wet and planted into a moist bed.

Pinching lower leaves off lettuce, cabbage family plants, and tomato transplants is normally a good idea. Do not pinch off the lower leaves of eggplant, peppers, or any vine crops. To protect young plants from cutworms, slugs, and snails, sprinkle a healthy amount of coffee grounds, crushed red pepper, or fireplace ashes around the plants after planting.

Enjoy your gardens and don't forget to feed the birds!

12

BUILD A SNOWMAN

JIM SYSKO

Jim Sysko is the engineer who led the team that built the world's
tallest snowman (113 feet 7½ inches) in Bethel, Maine, in 1999.

Knowledge of snow type is the first thing to consider when making a snowman. Warm and sticky snow with good water content works best for rolling those small snowballs into the big snow boulders used in a classical, three-ball snowman. But if you have cold, dry snow, other methods are needed.

MAKING A REALLY BIG SNOWMAN

When we made the big record-setting guy back in 1999, we had no choice but to use the snow as it was. Sometimes it was cold, powdery, and dry; sometimes it was melting, wet, and slushy. I knew the only way we could effectively use snow of any condition was to put it in a mold. To make balls the traditional way in hopes of breaking the world record, which at the time was 96 feet, would have meant somehow rolling a ball at least 40 feet in diameter weighing a half-million pounds. Such a ball would never have stayed together or been able to support a smaller second ball on it and a third, head ball on top of that!

So we (about sixty volunteers) filled a 4-foot-high plywood

mold 80 feet in diameter with snow, stomped it down with our feet, and, after taking one piece of plywood out, moved the slightly smaller mold up on top of the first layer to cast the next one. Like making a layered wedding cake, we repeated this process until we were well over 100 feet in the air. We had to resort to a crane with a clamshell bucket to get snow up to the higher levels, but the hand spreading and foot packing continued until the end.

You too can use this mold process for smaller snowmen if the snow is too dry to roll. Dry, loose snow will quickly turn into a dense solid concretelike substance under the weight of additional layers, especially if the sun has a chance to work on it. It's like making your own glacier.

MAKING A NORMAL-SIZED CLASSIC SNOWMAN

ASSESSING THE SNOW

If the snow depth is 2 inches or less, don't attempt to make your snowman too big. A 5-foot-tall snowman can be made from a 2-inch-deep snow cover using only an area of about 20 feet by 20 feet. If the snow is deeper and you have lots of help, try a 7- or 8-foot snowman.

GEOGRAPHY

Assuming you have good sticky snow, start by selecting a spot for the snowman that is in the geographical center of the area of snow you will be rolling. Put him in the shade for longest "life."

ROLLING SNOW

Start by rolling the first ball around the outside of the area, gradually tending toward the middle, all the while making it as round as possible for easier rolling. When it's big enough or you can't roll it anymore, brace this ball by packing lots of snow around its base. Roll the second and third balls, remembering that dense snow can be heavy, so be careful when lifting these. Recruit friends to help—the more hands the better! If you are building with a small group, use a wide wooden plank as an inclined ramp to roll or slide your snowballs up.

LONGEVITY

Pack bracing snow at the belt line and neck to keep the guy together. If you want the face to last as long as possible, carve and create the features on the side of the head away from the sun. You will likely want to show off your creation so place and face your snowman in the direction that gets the most visibility.

Dress him up, and if you have the time and ambition, make a whole family to keep him company. Remember that snowmen usually don't last long in this world, except in our memories, so treat them well. Snowmen have a way of paying us back by making us all a little younger.

13

MAKE HOT CHOCOLATE

Maury Rubin

Maury Rubin is a pastry chef and owner of The City Bakery *in New York City and Los Angeles. He is the author of* Book of Tarts: Form, Function, and Flavor at the City Bakery *and the creator of* The City Bakery Annual Hot Chocolate Festival.

To make great hot chocolate, you must cross the Hot Chocolate Divide (HCD).

The HCD, as it were, constitutes the difference between making hot chocolate with cocoa powder and making it with actual chocolate. The difference is akin to crossing the Atlantic in a canoe as opposed to a luxury liner. While cocoa powder was the limp but prime ingredient of nearly all hot chocolate made *last* century, actual chocolate has become the standard in these heady hot chocolate times of the *new* century. For those somehow still functioning in a hot chocolate world based on cocoa powder, are you aware that (1) we've walked on the moon and (2) if your rotary telephone breaks, repair service may be difficult to find?

I realize that by reducing a principle as important as the Hot Chocolate Divide to three measly letters—HCD—there is the risk of trivializing its importance. Please don't be misled: in the world of hot chocolate—a world where winter bellies are warmed, children made to stop crying, and gustatory dreams actually come true—the HCD is as real and tangible as the San Andreas fault.

Assuming, then, you accept this proposition, let's address the matter of "actual chocolate." Actual chocolate means a bar of chocolate, be it a bar of fine dark chocolate, elegant and smooth with a likely European pedigree, or even a weak and waxy slab of processed chocolate that tumbled into your possession from a vending machine. In either scenario, you've got the goods to get started.

The objective is simply to melt the chocolate bar down with only as much liquid as necessary to transform your chocolate "bar" to chocolate "drink." There are several choices on the liquid front: water, milk, cream, or even wine (a luscious Syrah, thank you very much, or better yet, a fortified wine such as Port). Any of these will work, and even a combination of them may do the trick with flair.

You don't need a specific recipe so much as a formula. We're after a rich and luscious sensory experience, so the basic approach is one part chocolate to one part liquid (weigh them on a small kitchen scale). If you're using dairy ingredients, try slightly more chocolate by weight. To make the hot chocolate, simply break the chocolate into 2-inch pieces and place it in a large bowl. Pour your liquid of choice into a medium saucepot. Heat only until the liquid is set to boil; then pour into the bowl of broken chocolate. Let sit exactly 1 minute and then stir to combine with a whisk. (Note: never do this in reverse; that is, never add the chocolate to the sauce pot of liquid, or it will sink to the bottom and instantly burn beyond recognition.)

Your hot chocolate is now ready, save for one suggestion: don't serve it too hot. Any hot chocolate expert would be much less than an expert, if failing to advise on the pitfalls of chocolate and heat. The fact is, chocolate doesn't love heat, especially fine chocolate. The ideal serving temperature for hot chocolate is 130 degrees Fahrenheit. At that temperature, if you've used quality chocolate and perhaps some of the more indulgent liquid options, then you'll be rewarded with the great pleasure of what hot chocolate in the twenty-first century should be.

14

DESIGN A FAMILY ROOM

GENEVIEVE GORDER

Genevieve Gorder is a designer and host of TLC's Town Haul
as well as a designer on Trading Spaces. *With her company,*
gg Studios, she works on a variety of projects ranging
from packaging design to interior decorating.

The family room has become a beige box but it doesn't have to stay this way. Rebel! A family room plays a defining role in our social lives and, as the first room people see in your home, carries the burden of creating many first impressions. With the following simple rules, you can easily design a room you enjoy spending time in with your family and friends.

DON'T FEAR CHANGE

While design can appear solely aesthetic from the outside, the process and result of the experience is extremely emotional. Not until you're truly ready to let go should you begin to get involved in any kind of renovation process big or small. To get a head start on the whole process, go in with the right knowledge—and keep in mind that this is not an exact science.

THINK ABOUT FUNCTION

A family room should combine form and function. It should make a statement but also provide a sacred space for your family. From formal plastic-wrapped couches that say "Don't sit here with your dirty pants or I will hunt you down" to the overstuffed "chofa" (sofa meets chair) that beckons you to simply come in and relax (I don't recommend either of these!), styles should always reflect the inhabitants.

FINDING YOUR INSPIRATION

Depending on the vibe you'd like to create, choose something tangible or sentimental that conjures up that feeling. For example, if you'd like to really make a family room inviting for conversation—and at the same time relaxing—think about what surrounds you at your favorite restaurant. If it's refuge you seek, what colors do you associate with these experiences? These details will define your design and will inspire you to create and complete the experience.

CALL YOUR MOTHER

While you could call your own mom if you loved her family room, I'm talking about a different Mother: Mother Nature. Think of Mother Nature as your personal design assistant. When you're looking to add color, one of the boldest, most cost-effective ways to impact a space, look to your local grocer or florist. No matter what the color, Mother Nature has made it and all you have to do is dissect. By cutting an apple in two, you have your creamy wall color (the meat), your stain (the seeds), and your accent pillows and throw (the skin).

USE YOUR FIVE SENSES

Take all five senses—sight, sound, touch, smell, and taste—into account when designing your space. Pull in patterns to add texture. Pluck fresh flowers to give the room scent. Employ diverse lighting styles to give the room added ambience. Music is key—use ambient music for a low key feel or some hip-hop for a livelier family room.

TURN OFF THE TV!

I know it sounds strange coming from me, but the television shouldn't be the focal point of your family room. The arrangement of your furniture and accessories will determine how the room is used. If you fill the room with a gigantic television, people will not feel inclined to talk to one another, and a family room, above all else, should inspire your family to communicate and spend time together. Find your focal point, a window or a fireplace, and place couches in an L-like arrangement or facing each other to inspire communication. By thinking intuitively and symmetrically, you'll give your room (and your family) what you've all yearned for, balance.

AVOID CLUTTER

Collections are conversation starters and also function as visual comfort food for you and your family's soul. When displaying these pieces, do not obsess. You don't have to pull out every single figurine and carefully place it in your grandma's hutch. Be selective. Choose the top ten pieces and really highlight them. With lighting and the right placement, they celebrate and personalize your family room.

THE FAM

After all of this work, you may feel as though you've created a masterpiece. While it may be a work of perfection, remember that you and your family should not only be able to look at it admiringly, you should love *living* in it. Use it! It's okay to have a mark on the wall, or a pillow out of place; this is what life looks like. No one can design that better than you and your family.

15

MAKE SPAGHETTI AND MEATBALLS

Giada De Laurentiis

Giada De Laurentiis is the host of Everyday Italian *on the Food Network. She is the author of* Everyday Italian: 125 Simple and Delicious Recipes. *De Laurentiis became a professional chef after attending the famed Le Cordon Bleu Culinary School in Paris.*

Spaghetti and meatballs is a classic Italian American dish and everyone has a favorite recipe. The traditional meat combination is pork, veal, and beef, but I like to make my meatballs with turkey. It's lighter, healthier, and that way I can eat it more often. The secret to making moist and juicy meatballs is to not overwork the mixture—combine all the ingredients together in a bowl and then add the meat and *gently* stir just until combined.

Turkey Meatballs
Makes about 3 dozen meatballs

¼ cup plain dried bread crumbs
¼ cup fresh chopped Italian parsley

2 large eggs, lightly beaten

2 tablespoons whole milk

¾ cup grated Romano cheese

¾ teaspoon salt

¾ teaspoon freshly ground black pepper

1 pound ground turkey, dark meat

¼ cup extra-virgin olive oil

5 cups jarred marinara sauce

In a large bowl, stir together the bread crumbs, parsley, eggs, milk, ½ cup of the cheese, and the salt and pepper. Add the turkey and gently stir to combine, being careful not to overwork the meat. Shape the meat mixture into bite-sized balls.

In a large skillet, heat the oil over a medium-high flame. Working in batches, add the meatballs and cook without moving or turning the meatballs until they are brown on the bottom, about 3 minutes. Turn the meatballs over and brown the other side, about 3 minutes longer. Continue to cook until all the sides are golden brown. Add the marinara sauce and bring to a boil. Reduce the heat and simmer until the flavors blend, about 5 minutes. The meatballs can be made up to this point 1 day ahead. Cool and then cover and refrigerate. (Rewarm before continuing.) Transfer the meatballs to a platter, reserving the extra sauce for the spaghetti. Sprinkle with the remaining cheese.

Cooking spaghetti is easy, but it's important that you cook the pasta in an ample amount of water so that it cooks evenly and doesn't stick together. And adding plenty of salt will help flavor the pasta.

Spaghetti
Makes 4 main-course servings

6 quarts water
¼ cup sea salt
1 pound dried pasta

Combine the water and salt in a large pot. Cover and bring the salt water to a boil over high heat. Add the pasta and cook until tender but still firm to the bite, stirring occasionally, about 8 minutes. Drain. Place the cooked spaghetti in a skillet with the remaining sauce and toss to coat. Transfer the pasta to a separate large serving bowl and serve with the meatballs.

Buon appetito!

16

HOST A HOUSEGUEST

PATRICK O'CONNELL

Patrick O'Connell is the proprietor of The Inn at Little

Washington. Located in Washington, Virginia, it is the first

establishment ever to receive five stars for both food and

accommodation by Mobil Travel Guide. O'Connell and

The Inn have received five James Beard awards, including

the Best Service award.

Spending the night in somebody else's home can be anxiety provoking. A good host is well aware of this and takes pains to ensure that his guests feel as comfortable as if they're staying in a luxury hotel but receiving the kind of pampering only friends can provide.

Entertaining is never effortless. The trick is to make it *appear* effortless. That requires careful planning, a great deal of thought, and meticulous organization. Sometimes good luck and a bit of magic are also helpful.

Have you spent the night in your guest room recently? It's surprising how few people actually do this. It's the best and easiest way to assess the room's shortcomings and see how one of your guests might feel staying in it. Some of the questions you should ask yourself include: How does it compare to staying in a good hotel? Is the bed large enough and comfortable? Are the linens of good quality? Is there an extra blanket and pillow in the closet? Does your guest room have ample closet and drawer space? Is there good light to read by? Is there a comfortable easy chair? Are there some good books and magazines tailored to the interests of your guests? Is there an alarm clock by the bedside? Will your window treatments block out unwanted light in the morning and offer privacy at night?

Bottled water and a small vase of flowers are a welcome addition by the bed or on the vanity in the bathroom. Be sure that special towels and soaps are laid out in the bathroom. A small basket containing miniature toiletries such as toothpaste, shaving cream, shampoo, and so on is a thoughtful touch in case a guest has forgotten something.

Snacks in the guest room are comforting and homey. If you know food or drink preferences, it's easier to delight someone. A small bowl of fruit, a plate of cookies, or a tin of nuts provides the nervous or perpetually hungry guest with something to munch on. A split of champagne or a half-bottle of wine add a festive touch. (Remember to include glasses and a wine opener.)

Try to pinpoint an expected guest's arrival time and be ready. Check the temperature in the house to be sure it's ideal. Soothing background music helps create a relaxed mood. A delectable aroma emanating from the kitchen is always enticing. Everything that can be accomplished in advance *should* be. This will allow you to be as relaxed as possible and able to focus all your attention on the guest.

Never attempt to cook a dish for the first time when you are entertaining, regardless of how simple it may seem. I recommend cooking the entire menu the week before for your family so that you can analyze how the food makes you feel. As a result, you may decide to add or delete a course or to increase or decrease a portion size. It is helpful to select china, serving platters, and utensils and lay them out in advance.

Tapping into your creativity during the planning process can be as pleasurable as the actual event. Think of yourself as a movie producer and visualize your celebration in advance as if you are seeing it on film. Identify the mood you would like to convey. Take time to dream about your perfect party.

After all, entertaining is simply about sharing your private world with others. What could be more fascinating than a glimpse into another person's reality or fantasy? It's better than the movies.

17

SHARPEN KNIVES

DANIEL BOULUD

Daniel Boulud is a renowned chef with restaurants in New York,

Palm Beach, and Las Vegas. He is the author of five books

and a regular column for Elle Decor *magazine. His line*

of kitchenware and knives, Daniel Boulud Kitchen (DBK),

was released in fall 2005.

I can tell so much about a cook simply by observing how he or she handles and maintains his or her knives. One of the most important things a young cook learns is to keep his knives well sharpened at all times. Proper sharpening affects your efficiency, speed, and accuracy and builds a foundation of overall respect for kitchen tools and equipment.

Having grown up on a farm, I was quite familiar with sharpening all kinds of tools by the time I reached the kitchen. I still have some old knives that date back as far as the first apprenticeship I did at the age of fourteen. The handles are so worn, they are practically molded to fit my grip. This makes them as comfortable and familiar as a favorite pair of old slippers, but I keep their blades as well sharpened as on the first day I got them. The details I have come to look for in professional cutlery include weight, balance, strong high-carbon stainless steel, and a comfortable handle.

STONE VERSUS STEEL

I am not a big fan of electric sharpeners as it is hard to control and fine-tune the usage. Electric sharpeners can help to get you on the right path for blades that have been allowed to become extremely dull, but it's still best to finish the job with a sharpening steel or stone.

To really sharpen a knife, you will need a sharpening stone and sharpening steel. In the simplest terms, you should use a stone for deep sharpening and a steel for everyday maintenance.

Use a stone when you need to bring back a truly dull knife edge. There are many types of stones, those used with water or with oil and those used dry. Your choice will depend on what makes you feel comfortable. I prefer a water stone as the water moderates the wearing effect of the stone and is cleaner to use than oil. The stone acts as an abrasive surface against which you refine a blade's edge. When sharpening with a stone, rub the knife's edge across the stone at an angle of 20 degrees.

A sharpening steel provides a broader edge that will need resharpening less often than with a stone. It has sharpening properties, but above all, it serves to realign a blade's edge, straightening any nicks, bumps, and warping that result from everyday use.

When using steel, follow these basic guidelines:

* Place your knife blade against the steel to form a 20-degree angle.
* Slide the entire length of your blade against the steel while exerting pressure on the knife blade. Repeat on both sides of the blade.
* Wipe the knife blade with a clean dish towel and then test its cutting edge. Repeat until the knife is satisfactorily sharp.

Here are a few more tips to keep your knives in top form:

* Choose the right knife for the right task. The sculpted edge of a boning knife will work its way around a poultry joint far more effectively than the broad blade of a chef's knife. Remember that your paring knife is not a screwdriver, and your serrated bread knife is not a saw.
* If you simply cannot resist using your chef's knife to crack open lobster claws, limit the damage by using the knife's spine, not the blade's edge.
* If you tend to cut using a forward motion with your knife moving away from you, do the same when you sharpen with a stone or steel.
* When buying a set of knives test the handle in your hand for weight, balance, and comfort.
* If you are buying your first knife set, or even just a single good knife, make sure to invest in a sharpening steel at the same time.

Treat your knives well and they will serve you well.

18

CARVE A TURKEY

ART SMITH

Art Smith is Oprah Winfrey's personal chef. He is
the best-selling author of two books, including Kitchen Life:
Real Food for Real Families—Even Yours!

For many of you, the memory of a family member carving a beautifully cooked turkey at the holiday table is as pleasant to recall as a Norman Rockwell painting. Unfortunately, my childhood memory of this event isn't as charming. I remember many overcooked holiday birds that resulted in a "turkey pull" instead of a traditional carving. This can be easily avoided with patience, some common sense, and practice.

Naturally, it is important to first cook a turkey properly to ensure a succulent, moist, and thoroughly cooked bird. The carving is equally important to maximize the amount of meat offered as well as a pleasurable dining experience.

The following are some helpful hints and steps:

* If you are carving soon after roasting, cover the turkey with foil and let it stand for 15 minutes first.
* Work in the kitchen—especially if it's your first time carving

a bird. Carving can make a mess if you're not careful and lack experience.

* Choose a sharp, thin-bladed carving knife.
* Cut dark meat before light meat, as it will stay moist longer.

THIGHS, LEGS, AND WINGS

Pull the legs away from the body of the turkey to allow the top of the thighbone to be seen. Cut the thighbone using a very sharp knife. Carefully slice the meat from the body along the lower torso. Then,

with the knuckle bone at the end of the drumstick pointed toward you, cut through the connecting joint at the drumstick and thigh to separate them. While holding the knucklebone, cut parallel slices through the tendons. Slice the thigh by cutting evenly and parallel to the bone.

By cutting between joints, and not through bones, you can disconnect bones without much fuss. If you do try to saw through a bone, even if your knife can do it, you'll take a long time and make a mess in the process.

THE TURKEY BREAST

Remove each half of the turkey breast by cutting along the bone at the keel, located at the top of the bone. I recommend using a longer knife blade to get into this area. It is important to take your time, have patience, and be very careful.

Once you have removed the breast

meat from the carcass, place the meat on a cutting board for slicing. Slice in long, horizontal cuts (parallel to the cutting board) toward the bottom of the breast while staying as close to the wing as you can until you reach the bottom. Your vertical cuts should meet this horizontal line. If you make thin, clean, even cuts, the meat should separate well.

19

HAVE PATIENCE

M. J. RYAN

M. J. Ryan is one of the creators of the best-selling Random
Acts of Kindness *series and the author of* The Power of
Patience *and* The Happiness Makeover, *among other titles.*
A contributing editor to Good Housekeeping, *she works with*
executives and other individuals who want to live
more satisfying and meaningful lives.

Doesn't it seem that the faster we go, the less patience we have?
This is problematic because life inevitably has a certain amount
of annoyances such as lines, traffic jams, and automated message
systems. More important, most of life's challenges—illness, dis-
ability, relationship conflicts, job crises, parenting issues—
require that we practice patience in great quantity.

We all need patience because it gives us self-control, the
capacity to stop and make wise choices. Patience helps us be
more loving toward others, more at ease with the circumstances
of our lives, and more able to get what we want.

Patience is a human quality that can be strengthened like a

muscle. With the right attitude and a bit of practice, you can learn to harness the power of patience. It's a combination of motivation (wanting to), awareness (paying attention to our inner landscape), and cultivation (practicing). You're patient already—how else did you get through school, learn to love, find a job? You're just not always aware of what triggers your impatience, or what to do when your patience wears thin.

Here's how to begin:

1. Do a study of what triggers your impatience. For me, it's inanimate objects and waiting in line.

2. Notice what happens right before you blow. It could be something you say to yourself, a movie you run in your head, a feeling in your body. For me, it's the phrase "I don't have time for this." When I say that, I feel the irritation and annoyance that is impatience.

3. Once you notice what you do, say, or see, do something to counteract it. For me, it's saying, "I have all the time I need." For you, it might be visualizing a peaceful scene or breathing slowly.

Here are ten other ways to harness patience when you need it:

1. Try laughing at yourself or the situation.

2. Think about how far you've come, not how much you have left to do.

3. Count to 10—or 100.

4. Put a pebble in your pocket and move it from one to the other when you notice yourself getting antsy. You'll interrupt the cycle.

5. Rather than nag, seek practical solutions to the things that irritate you. Get a refrigerator with an automatic ice-cube maker if you

go nuts about your sweetie's always forgetting to fill the ice-cube trays; get the toothpaste that comes in a pump if you see red at the sight of the cap left off.

6. When forced to wait, visualize the most peaceful place you can think of. See, feel, and hear yourself there. Bring to mind the feelings that such a place evokes in you. Relish this chance to take a little daydream to Tahiti or the Alps.

7. Use a red light, ringing phone, or other frustration to notice three breaths. Simply notice how your breath goes in and comes out, without trying to change it.

8. Reduce or swear off caffeine. Caffeine is a stimulant that can cause jitteriness and irritability, the inability to take life in stride.

9. Would I rather be right or effective? That's a great question to hold in your mind when you're in a conflict with someone.

10. Ask for help. There's no prize at the end of your life for doing too much, particularly if you do it in a frazzled state.

TO PROTECT

20

SECURE YOUR HOME

AL CORBI

Al Corbi created the science of modern-day ballistic-resistant security for residences, corporate headquarters, and superyachts. For thirty-four years, he has been designing the ultimate security systems around the world.

Before your family can be truly safe in your home, it is essential to understand what residential security can be as well as what it is not.

THE MYTHS

HOME IS A SAFE PLACE

Most homes, even gated communities and estate properties, provide little genuine protection. Home invasions are the least risky, most lucrative activity for criminals. In addition to the life-threatening home invasion, 60 percent of all rapes and 35 percent of all assaults occur during home invasions.

BURGLAR ALARMS PROTECT US

Burglar alarms make noise, not security. By the time your alarm goes off, a determined criminal is already in your home.

Alarms do nothing to protect those inside at the time of the break-in.

THE POLICE WILL INTERVENE

Assuming the police respond, it typically takes up to 30 minutes or more. Any crime that is going to happen is most likely going to take place in the first 15 minutes.

SECURITY GUARDS ARE THE ANSWER FOR HIGH-RISK FAMILIES

Even armed guards are vulnerable to an attack. No one wins in a fight; there are only varying degrees of loss. Time, however, eventually neutralizes any threat, whereas force raises the stakes. At the heart of any effective security system is the principle of isolation, having a protected interior space where your family is safe.

THE SOLUTIONS

There are effective home security solutions for every financial and safety consideration. What follows will direct you to the best technique for your needs.

RULE 1: CRIMINALS DO NOT WANT TO BE DETECTED

For less than the cost of six months of monitoring fees, you can do something that truly adds to your safely. Install exterior motion detector lighting around your home, which activates when the criminal steps foot on your property. It is the lights of the motion detector that alarms the would-be intruder to the fact that he is being watched. It is important that other lights are not left on; these simply illuminate the criminal's path.

RULE 2: CRIMINALS DO NOT WANT TO GO TO JAIL

A picture is worth a thousand words, or dollars to a lawyer in this case. A $150 surveillance system can provide necessary evidence for catching and prosecuting a criminal. Proof is no longer exclusive to the rich and powerful.

RULE 3: NO ONE WILL BE THERE TO HELP YOU WHEN THE CRIME OCCURS
When an intruder enters your home it is only about you and him for the next 30 minutes. It doesn't matter if your alarm has sent a signal to the monitoring station or if the police are on their way. Make arrangements now to safely and effectively isolate your family from an intruder until police arrive. If you don't, you and your family risk being victims. When the police do arrive, they will most probably take a report about the crime that has just devastated your family.

RULE 4: HIDING IN A CLOSET OR UNDER A BED DOES NOT PROTECT YOU
Instead:

1. Make your property as uninviting to a would-be criminal as possible with lights and sound.
2. Fortify exterior doors and windows with effective locking systems. Day or night, at home or away, always keep your windows and doors locked.
3. Create an interior area that isolates your family from a threat.

Criminals choose their victims. Don't be one. None of the above will stop a crime, but it will move the criminal to someone else's home who didn't take this advice.

21

PREVENT IDENTITY THEFT

SENATOR DIANNE FEINSTEIN

Senator Dianne Feinstein is the senior senator from California
and author of a law that increases federal penalties for
serious incidences of identity theft.

Chances are good that you or someone you know has been a victim of identity theft. The Federal Trade Commission (FTC) estimates that 10 million Americans are victims of this crime each year. And this number is growing every day.

Identity theft can happen in so many ways: A thief can steal your credit cards. Or buy your social security number online. Or purchase cell phones, automobiles, or houses in your name.

Here are some steps you can take to prevent your identity from being stolen:

* *Be vigilant in protecting your personal information—especially your driver's license, social security number, and credit card numbers.* These are known as "breeder documents" and are the keys to your identity.
* *Make copies of the contents of your purse or wallet.* This will help you in the event of a loss or theft.

* *Check your credit report at least once a year.* This will ensure that credit cards are not opened in your name.
* *Tear up or shred bank and credit statements, as well as "junk mail" credit card offers.* Thieves will sift through your garbage and sign up for the offers in your name.
* *Never allow your bank to put your social security number or driver's license number on your checks.* This just makes it easier for identity thieves to steal your personal information.
* *Never give out your personal information over the phone* unless you initiate the call or verify that it is a legitimate business.
* *Never provide or update personal information in response to e-mail requests.* This practice is a scam designed solely to obtain your most personal information.
* *Write your congressman and senators.* Let them know that you think we need stronger laws to protect your personal information from identity theft.

Here is what you should do if your identity is stolen:

* *Contact the fraud departments of any one of the three major credit agencies.* This will ensure that creditors contact you when someone tries to open a new account or change personal information on your existing accounts. When one of the agencies (Equifax, Experian, or Trans Union) confirms the fraud alert, the other agencies will be notified, and they will send you a free copy of your credit report.
  Equifax: 800-525-6285
  Experian: 888-397-3742
  Trans Union: 800-680-7289
* *Cancel your credit cards immediately if your purse or wallet is stolen.*

Instruct your credit card company to flag your account with a fraud alert.

* *File a police report.* You may be required to show proof that your identity was stolen at a later date.
* *File a complaint with the Federal Trade Commission.* This helps track incidents of identity theft and helps investigators break major fraud rings.

Identity theft is serious business. When your identity is stolen, you must spend valuable time and energy trying to restore your good name and, sometimes more important, your good credit rating.

It takes the average victim roughly two years and as much as $18,000 to recover their identity. So guard your personal information carefully, and do everything you can to prevent your identity from being stolen.

22

PRACTICE HOME FIRE SAFETY

RYAN SUTTER

Ryan Sutter is a firefighter in Vail, Colorado. He is also known
for his starring role in ABC's reality series The Bachelorette.
His wedding to Trista Rehn was filmed by ABC
and watched by millions of viewers.

HOW FIRES START

In order for a fire to start and sustain itself, it needs three basic ingredients: oxygen, fuel, and heat. Removing any one of the three results in either the inability of a fire to ignite or the extinguishment of an already existing fire. It is the homeowner's responsibility to make sure that all three are not present in potentially fire-causing proximity. Since humans and pets need oxygen, it is important to focus on the potentially hazardous sources of fuel and heat throughout the house.

HOW TO PREVENT A FIRE

Take a look around your home. Do you have candles near curtains, boxes against heaters, or overloaded electrical outlets? Have you left the stove on or the iron plugged in? Anything that produces heat or electricity near flammable material is a fire threat. Most home fires start from careless errors and could be prevented by taking a few moments to look around the house.

In certain areas, such as kitchens, garages, or workshops, however, it may be more difficult to effectively separate heat and fuel sources. In places like the kitchen, small amounts of fire and heat are necessary so they are more susceptible and it is a good idea to have fire extinguishers readily accessible within them. It is key to select the appropriate extinguisher for its intended use. By law, all fire extinguishers must be rated and labeled with the type and size fire they may be used on. Unless the fire is small and can be easily contained with an extinguisher, evacuate your home and call 911.

Most homes are equipped with gas and water shut-offs as well as electric fuse boxes. Everyone in the home should know how to access and operate these shut-offs in case of an emergency. A leak or short in any one of these can be dangerous so it is important that each of these be accurately labeled and accessible. Easy access and proper labeling will serve not only as an effective way to prevent a fire but will allow the fire department to work more quickly should a fire start in the home.

Most people are familiar with or own home smoke detectors. Fewer people are aware of the importance of additional carbon monoxide (CO) detectors. Still fewer properly implement and maintain any of the detectors in their home. Smoke and CO detectors are critical in the swift notification of fire danger. They should be in every room where people sleep as well as in higher risk areas like the kitchen, workshops, or garage. They should be tested and batteries replaced every six months. A good rule of thumb is to change the batteries and test your detectors when you change clocks for daylight savings.

HOW TO HANDLE A FIRE

Even in the most well-informed and well-intentioned homes, mistakes happen and fires can start. At this point, a home is just a house. The concern is no longer on the prevention of its loss, but on the preservation of the lives within. Quick and accurate notification and efficient escape are essential. Evacuation routes and an exterior meeting place should be established and practiced at least once annually.

Sleeping at night should be done with bedroom doors shut. If a fire does start while you are sleeping, feel the closed door with the back of your hand before exiting. A hot door or doorknob means that fire or extremely hot conditions exist just outside your door. It is not safe for you to leave through that door. If you sleep on the ground floor or have a fire escape from the window, exit through the window. If neither of these is an option, dial 911 and inform the dispatchers of your location. Remain calm and low to the ground. Hang a sheet out your window to signal firefighters and listen for their arrival.

If the proper precautions have been taken, then the chances of being trapped in a burning home are slim. If an alarm sounds, get out and call 911. Do not try to take anything with you, and never return to a burning building. The fire department is trained to do everything it can for your home and will make every effort to preserve what they can. Firefighters know, as you should too, that no home or property is more valuable than a life.

23

MAINTAIN A HEALTHY REFRIGERATOR

CAROLYN O'NEIL

Carolyn O'Neil is co-author of The Dish on Eating Healthy and Being Fabulous! *She is a registered dietician and former host of CNN's* On the Menu *and* Travel Now.

What's in your refrigerator? If you answer, "A bottle of chardonnay, two light beers, four kinds of salad dressing, and a few restaurant ketchup packets," then we've got to talk. While it's not necessary to create a scene worthy of "Fridge Styles of the Rich and Famous," what you have on hand will dictate what you'll nosh, especially when you want to eat *now!* So, to help you better stock your cold storage, here is a primer on ice-box basics.

I recommend prioritizing fresh fruit and vegetable storage. When you bring produce home from the market, get it ready for future dinner times right away. For instance, wash and trim celery so you can grab a stalk when you're in a hurry to munch. If they're easier to eat and cook, chances are you'll consume them!

THINK OUTSIDE THE BOX

Some produce just doesn't fare well in the fridge. Avocados, bananas, potatoes, onions, and tomatoes, for example, don't like to be too cold. Even strawberries, which should be refrigerated to stay fresh, taste more fragrant if you let them return to room temperature before eating.

THE RAW TRUTH

Keep your fresh veggies and raw meats away from each other. If bacteria-laden meat and chicken juices drip onto salad greens, you're asking for big tummy trouble. Store raw meats in sealable plastic bags and put them in the solitary confinement of the refrigerator's meat drawer. Wipe up any spills of raw meat juices with a paper towel rather than a sponge, so you can throw it away after cleaning the refrigerator.

EASY CHICKS

Keep bags of frozen chicken breasts on hand for healthy dinners in a hurry. They're IQF products, which stands for "individually quick frozen," so they don't stick together. Brush on some olive oil, season with your favorite herbs, and cook according to package directions.

WANT A COLD ONE?

If you stand there staring into an open fridge, the temperature is going to go up and foods won't last as long. Shut the refrigerator! When it is closed, the warmest spot is the shelf area on the door, so that's a good place to store relatively long-life foods like mustards, salsas, and pickles. The coldest spot is near the bottom, that's why the meat drawer is there. The crisper drawer has a higher humidity level to help keep fresh veggies from wilting. So store things accordingly.

Bad bacteria love warm temperatures—so give them the big chill! Whether it's leftovers from dinner or the foods on your cookout buffet, you shouldn't leave cooked foods out at room temperature for more than 2 hours. If you're outside and it's hotter than 90 degrees Fahrenheit, you shouldn't leave them out any longer than 1 hour. Buy a refrigerator thermometer to make sure temps stay below 40 degrees Fahrenheit.

IT'S BETTER TO BE SHALLOW

When putting away cooked foods that are still hot, make sure to store them in shallow containers so that they can cool more quickly to below 40 degrees Fahrenheit. If you put a big pot of hot chili in the fridge, it can take a really long time to get chilly.

SHOULD IT STAY OR SHOULD IT GO?*

PRODUCT	REFRIGERATION	FREEZER
Fresh eggs, in shell	3–5 weeks	Don't freeze
Hard-boiled eggs	1 week	Don't freeze
Luncheon meats, opened	3–5 days	1–2 months
Luncheon meats, unopened	2 weeks	1–2 months
Steaks, roasts, or chops	3–5 days	4–12 months
Cooked meat and meat casseroles	3–4 days	2–3 months
Chicken or turkey, pieces	1–2 days	9 months
Cooked poultry casseroles	3–4 days	4–6 months
Juices in cartons	3 weeks, unopened	8–12 months
	7–10 days, opened	
Hard cheese	6 months, unopened	6 months
	3–4 weeks, opened	
Soft cheese	1 week	6 months
Margarine	4–5 months	12 months
Butter	1–3 months	6–9 months

PRODUCT	REFRIGERATION	FREEZER
Milk	7 days	3 months
Yogurt	7–14 days	1–2 months
Fresh fish	1–2 days	2–3 months
Shellfish	1–2 days	3–6 months
Cooked shellfish	3–4 days	3 months

* From www.foodsafety.gov

LEFTOVER LOVE

Reheat all leftovers to 165 degrees Fahrenheit, until hot and steaming. Don't have a clue how long leftovers have been in the fridge? When in doubt, throw it out! You're better off safe than sick.

24

INCORPORATE FITNESS INTO YOUR DAILY LIFE

JORGE CRUISE

Jorge Cruise is the exclusive weight-loss coach for AOL and

coaches more than 3 million online clients through his website.

He is the FitSmart columnist for USA WEEKEND *magazine*

and The New York Times *best-selling author of* 8 Minutes

in the Morning® *and* The 3-Hour Diet.™

The biggest fitness challenge is finding time for an exercise routine. The good news is that to maintain health even small amounts of action from everyday activities can get it done. Here are my recommendations for general health, training, and weight loss.

SET A GOAL

You're more likely to stick with your plan if you have a goal. Do you want to lose weight? Lower your blood pressure? Complete a physical challenge? Be specific and write it down, such as "lose 10 pounds in 90 days."

MAKE A PLAN

How much time do you have and what's realistic? Six 5-minute bursts of activity are as good as a single 30-minute block if your goal is basic health. However, if you're training for an event, you've got to schedule training sessions. Take that sheet of paper stating your goal, and add your plan, for example, "Leave my desk and walk around the building for 10 minutes at 10 A.M., noon, and 3 P.M. daily" or "Complete two long runs, two hill runs, and two easy runs each week."

FIND THE RIGHT TIME

To achieve results beyond general health, you've got to schedule workouts like you would a meeting. Research shows people who exercise in the morning are more likely to stick with it, most likely because they get it out of the way before the chores of the day interfere. But it's important to enjoy your exercise; if you're miserable working out in the morning you won't do it. Try different times of day and keep a log of how you feel before and after the workout. Pick the time that works for you, put it in your planner, and stick with it.

PICK YOUR PROGRAM

The most efficient exercise for weight loss is strength training. Hours on the treadmill won't build the lean muscle that is essential to increasing resting metabolism. As few as 8 minutes a day of resistance training will do the trick. Work two different muscle groups to fatigue each day by doing three to four sets of two moves, back-to-back without resting. That way you don't waste time standing between sets. By the end of the week, you'll hit every muscle group. For a great home workout, buy an exercise band at any sporting goods store; they usually come with suggested moves for each body part. And to be safe, check with your doctor before you begin any new exercise program.

Here are two of my favorite moves to help you get started:

* *Lift-up hold (butt):* While lying on your back, bend knees and place feet flat on floor. Exhale as you lift hips as high as you can; try to form a straight line from shoulders to knees. Hold for 2 counts and inhale as you slowly lower almost to mat. Repeat 12 times.
* *Superman (back):* Lie with belly on floor, legs straight and arms extended in front. Looking at floor, exhale and lift arms and legs about 4 inches off the ground. Hold for 2 seconds. Inhale while slowly lowering to start position. Repeat 12 times.

Make everyday activities count:

* *Don't use the drive-up window for the bank, fast-food, coffee, or dry cleaning.* Park the car far away and walk.
* *Do squats.* These can be done while you're on the phone at work or home, or while watching TV.
* *Do active chores daily.* Shovel snow (432 calories/hour), rake leaves (288 calories/hour), push a manual mower (396 calories/hour), or vacuum (239 calories/hour).

Finally, keep an activity log for a week. Write down the times you start and stop any activity. Add up the time at the end of each day; if you hit 30 minutes daily, you're on your way.

25

PREVENT HOUSEHOLD PESTS

GLEN ROLLINS

*Glen Rollins is the president and COO of Orkin, Inc., the
104-year-old pest control company. He began working for the
company as a summer intern when he was fourteen years old.*

While insects and other pests play an essential role in our environment, they can cause problems for homeowners. Whether they feed on you, your pets, or your personal assets, some pests can seriously jeopardize your health, home, and property.

These are some of the more common dangers and health risks associated with various household pests:

1. Cockroaches contaminate food and have been linked to asthma, especially in children.
2. Fire ants, among all types of ants, cause painful stings and crop devastation.
3. Spiders inflict painful bites. The brown recluse and black widow spiders are the most dangerous, causing pain and sometimes death.
4. Mosquitoes inflict uncomfortable bites and can transmit serious disease.

5. Flying/stinging insects such as bees, yellow jackets, and wasps inflict painful stings that can send people to hospitals for treatment.

6. House flies are the most prolific disease vectors in the world, carrying diseases such as typhoid fever, cholera, and dysentery.

7. Ticks are disease-carriers transmitting Lyme disease, Rocky Mountain spotted fever, and encephalitis.

8. Bed bugs inflict sometimes painful bites which leave itchy, bloody welts on skin and can cause allergic reactions.

CONDUCIVE CONDITIONS

While the treatment of pests should generally be left to professionals, there are a few basics to pest prevention that every homeowner should know. Understanding and eliminating elements that attract pests is key to prevention. The following three elements are essential to pest survival, so they should be minimized or eliminated entirely in your home:

1. *Moisture:* This includes standing rainwater, drainage, and condensation under or around a home. Areas you may not realize attract moisture:
   * Standing water in gutters can provide an attractive breeding ground.
   * Houses rained on during construction can take up to two years to dry completely. This provides a moisture source for pests and also supports mold growth.
   * Pipes form condensation around them when the water in them is a different temperature from the ambient temperature.

2. *Food:* This includes everything from wood framing, mulch, and human food to garbage, dust, and human hair.
   * Rodents will eat almost anything.

* Flies will eat dead blood and tissue, while bed bugs, fleas, ticks, and mosquitoes prefer live blood.
* Ants, bees, and yellow jackets prefer sweets, whereas cockroaches will eat any crumbs or garbage.

3. *Access:* Pests can find access to the inside of your home through tiny cracks in any material, including:
   * Wood brought inside to burn
   * Luggage from a trip, which can harbor bedbugs
   * Plants brought inside for the winter—even Christmas trees

PREVENTION TIPS

1. Remove unnecessary food and water sources in and around your home. Water pooling around an air conditioner or in flowerpots, toys, and birdbaths are all great sources for bugs. Do not leave food on counters and don't take food all over the house—a pest problem can easily spread throughout the house this way.

2. Clean your yard. Do not let branches, plants, bushes, mulch, or stacks of firewood provide pests with a highway to your home.

3. Store all food, including pet food and garbage, in sealed plastic containers. Insects and rodents can enter paper or cardboard containers relatively unnoticed. Storing flour, sugar, and other dry kitchen items in the refrigerator is another way to keep pantry pests at bay. Inspect all food brought into your home before storing.

4. Store indoor garbage containers in dry areas away from sites that can provide shelter for pests—not under the kitchen sink—and empty containers often. Keep external garbage cans away from your home.

5. Seal all cracks and crevices—no matter how small—with screen, caulk, or a copper version of steel wool. Many pests can fit their

entire bodies through the tiniest of holes. A rat can enter the home through an opening as small as a quarter, while a mouse can squeeze through a hole smaller than a dime.

6. Fit screens and tighten seals properly on doors and windows. If you're not sure if you've got good seals, check for spiders lurking in corners nearby. Spiders can detect the slightest intake of air caused by a crack or improper seal, so they will camp out in areas where insects can enter your home and wait there for their next meal. If you've got spiders, you've almost certainly got other insects.

7. Install weather strips at the bottom of exterior doors.

8. Vacuuming regularly removes adult pests as well as the eggs they lay.

9. Remove shelter sites such as cardboard boxes, paper grocery bags, and piles of newspapers or magazines. Cockroaches love these types of shelters, and they often ride home with you from the store in paper bags or boxes.

10. Once pests move into your home, they can be very difficult to remove. Contact a pest control professional to treat pest infestations.

Effective pest control not only safeguards property, but it also protects people's health and increases their well-being.

26

DUST

HELOISE

Heloise was selected as this book's only repeat expert from
The Experts' Guide to 100 Things Everyone Should Know
How to Do. *She is a columnist for* Good Housekeeping *and*
international syndication. She is the author of numerous books,
including Heloise to the Rescue: 1,245 Household
Problems Solved from Basement to Attic.

Dust, dust, go away, don't come back today. But, alas, it always does. Dust is a fine dry powder made of particles from the earth (or waste matter) picked up from the ground and carried through the air—until it lands in our homes. Even if you lived in a "sealed" environment, with other people or animals, dust would be present because dead skin, hair, particles, and even lint from clothes shedding contribute to the makeup of dust.

Where you live and the time of year usually determine how much dust accumulates in your home. Although dust can't be totally eliminated, it can be minimized by closing windows, shutting outside doors quickly, and keeping inside doors closed to help contain the spread of dust.

When you do a thorough dusting, don't just move it around; remove it. A feather duster or dry cloth will simply rearrange the dust and move it into the air. Depending on the surface, you will need to use a slightly damp cloth, a furniture polish, or a multipurpose spray cleaner in order to pick up and hold the dust. I put old, clean socks over my hands and spray them with furniture polish and dust away. I also love microfiber cloths because they capture dust without needing cleaning agents. They do a great job of removing dust from computer screens, furniture—and even pets. Electrostatically charged disposable cloths and quick-cleaning wipes are effective, too.

To control dust, start from the top down and take these steps:

* Every month, dust, clean, or change the air filters in air-conditioning and heating units. This can make a big difference (the more dust the filter traps, the less in your home).
* Wipe off windowsills often to stop the dust from getting further inside.
* With a long-handled brush, eliminate the dust and grime from ceiling fans and vacuum up any gunk that may have fallen to the floor.
* Vacuum the tops of china cabinets, bookcases, and armoires and then polish the surfaces. And don't forget moldings and baseboards.
* Regularly vacuum (with the brush attachment) louvered doors, pleated lampshades, and knickknacks.
* Wipe down kitchen and bathroom surfaces daily to get rid of dust and grease, which spread throughout the house. Then clean thoroughly once a week.
* Stand in the center of the room and look at all the surfaces—coffee tables, the dining room table, side tables, and nightstands. During

the week, do a 5-minute quick dust and polish. My mother called this "top cleaning."
* Many drapes and curtains can simply be put into the dryer for several minutes on the air setting to remove dust. A clean, new paintbrush can be used to dust miniblinds.
* Electronic and high-tech equipment—computers, TVs, DVDs, stereos—are magnets for dust. Wipe gently with microfiber cloths.
* Wash bedding (sheets, pillows, pillowcases, mattress covers, comforters) and washable rugs often, so dust mites don't nestle in them.
* If you have wall-to-wall carpeting (which traps dust), vacuum it frequently. Do the same for upholstered furniture. Have large area rugs professionally cleaned at least once a year.
* Sweep or vacuum first, then damp-mop linoleum, tile, or hardwood floors weekly.
* Check under furniture, in corners and closets to get rid of dust bunnies. Use a long-handled, dampened dust mop or vacuum attachment.

OTHER HELPFUL HINTS
* Keep your house dry. Dust mites thrive in humid conditions.
* Be mindful that window fans draw dust and dirt inside.
* Turning on the air conditioning helps to prevent dust from getting inside. Air purifiers with HEPA filters can remove some dust particles.
* Put doormats in front of every entrance to your home to collect dust and dirt before they are tracked inside.
* Sweep the sidewalk, driveway, and outside entryways.

Though you can't conquer dust, you can control it day by day.

27

REDUCE INDOOR AIR POLLUTION

JEFFREY HOLLENDER

Jeffrey Hollender is founder and CEO of Seventh Generation,

the nation's leading brand of nontoxic and environmentally safe

household products. He is the author of What Matters Most.

M ost people are shocked to learn that the air inside their homes is likely dirtier than the air outside. In spite of how unlikely it might seem, EPA research has shown that the atmosphere inside the average house contains levels of pollutants two to five times higher than levels found in nearby outdoor air. Some 900 different pollutants have been identified in indoor air, and five basic factors combine in various ways to put and keep them there.

1. Pesticides, household cleaners, toiletries, deodorizers, and other consumer chemical products introduce a wide variety of pollutants to our air when used.
2. Synthetic materials like the carpets, foams, insulation, and pressed wood products used to construct and furnish our homes release toxic fumes as the compounds they're made from break down with age.
3. Household combustion equipment like furnaces, water

heaters, and gas ranges add soot and a host of toxic gases to indoor air when improperly vented.

4. Drafty older homes in areas with higher levels of outdoor air pollution let that pollution seep inside.

5. Energy-efficient construction techniques create airtight living environments. Once pollutants arrive, they tend to stay and increase their concentrations over time.

Fortunately, there are plenty of things you can do to prevent or reduce indoor air pollution at home. Here are the those that will give you the biggest breathing bang for the buck:

* Unless you live in a highly polluted area, ventilate your home frequently. Open doors and windows wide to let good fresh air in and bad old air out—even in winter! The health benefits will far outweigh any added energy expense.

* Don't use synthetic cleaning, personal care, or other household chemical products. These add countless dangerous toxins to your home's air when used. Use only natural, nontoxic ingredient–based alternatives instead.

* Don't use synthetic air fresheners, deodorizers, or similar products. Substitute fresh air and natural essential oils.

* Never use chemical pesticides or herbicides in or around your home. This includes flea collars and treatments and similar pet products.

* Use a chlorine-free dishwasher detergent, and if you have chlorinated water install a showerhead filter. These prevent hot water–volatized chlorine vapors from entering your home.

* Have devices that create fire inspected annually to ensure they're properly vented. This list includes fireplaces, woodstoves, gas ranges and dryers, water heaters, and furnaces. Use only electric

space heaters. When buying new combustion-based appliances, don't buy any that employ a pilot light.

* Grow plants, which act as natural air scrubbers. Particularly effective species include Boston fern, palms, and rubber plants.
* Forbid smoking in your house.
* Use only beeswax and vegetable wax candles with metal-free cloth wicks and natural essential oil scents.
* Don't buy furniture or fixtures made from plywood, particleboard, of other composite pressed woods. Choose solid-wood items instead.
* Clean humidifiers and air conditioners frequently to prevent them from spreading molds and bacteria.
* Test your basement for radon, an invisible, odorless, natural radioactive gas that can seep in from the ground.
* Before installing new carpets, make sure they are free of volatile organic compounds, then air them out for at least a week unrolled or very loosely rolled in the garage or another outdoor space before bringing them inside. Use mechanical means like tacks rather than adhesives to install them. Once installed, keep fresh air circulating through the room for a year to remove the gases emitted by new carpet.
* Make your next vacuum cleaner a HEPA model, which will trap and permanently remove particulates, dust, and allergens instead of simply spewing them back out into the air like other machines.

28

STOCK YOUR MEDICINE CABINET

ISADORE ROSENFELD

Dr. Isadore Rosenfeld is the health editor for Parade *magazine and a medical consultant for FOX News. Rosenfeld is the author of fourteen books, seven of which are best-sellers, including* Dr. Isadore Rosenfeld's Breakthrough Health. *He is an attending physician at New York Hospital and the Rossi Distinguished Professor of Clinical Medicine at New York Hospital Weil Cornell Medical Center. Rosenfeld was appointed by President Bush to the Advising Committee of the White House Conference on Aging.*

Much of what you include in your medicine chest depends on the age and state of health of those living in your home. However, there are some basic supplies that everyone needs in order to cope with minor injuries and common, transient symptoms.

As important as what supplies to stock is where and how to keep them. Most medications lose some of their potency at high temperature and humidity. That's why you should no more keep them in your bathroom or kitchen than you would fine wine. Store them in a cool, dry, dark place such as a closet that's easily accessible to you but out of reach of your kids.

Now is a good time to clean out your medicine chest and make a fresh start. Don't put any discarded items into the wastebasket, where kids can get hold of them; flush them down the toilet.

* Throw out all expired prescription drugs.
* Get rid of any eyedroppers that touched the eyes when they were used.
* Discard bottles of partially used liquid medication that was swigged out of the bottle.
* Syrup of ipecac, which causes vomiting, used to be "indispensable" for poisoning. Stock activated charcoal instead.
* Mercury is toxic. Say goodbye to your mercury thermometer. It was never a good idea to put glass in anyone's mouth, anyway, especially kids'. Buy one of the new digital thermometers; the less expensive ones are just as accurate as the more costly type. Mercury can be dangerous, so don't throw it into the garbage. Take the old thermometer to a special collection center in your community.

You are now ready to stock up anew. Here's what you should have in addition to the prescription drugs your family needs:

* Bandages. Include a couple that are elastic to be used for strains.
* Scissors
* Adhesive tape
* Gauze
* Tweezers. If you hike in the woods, have a thin-tipped set, as well, to pick out ticks. Remember to clean your tweezers with alcohol before each use.

* Digital thermometer
* Rubbing alcohol
* Ice bag
* Heating pad
* Cotton balls and swabs
* Calibrated medicine spoon (to measure the exact dosage)

Now for the over-the-counter medications:

* *Pain:* Aspirin is the old standby (but never give it to anyone under age 18 who has a respiratory or other viral illness); acetaminophen (Tylenol); one of the nonsteroidal anti-inflammatory drugs such as naproxen (Aleve) or ibuprofen (Motrin). Remember, however, that these should not be taken in doses larger than what is indicated on the label and usually for no more than 10 consecutive days.
* *Indigestion:* Antacids. Liquid preparations act faster than the pills.
* *Occasional diarrhea:* Imodium, Lomotil, or Pepto-Bismol will usually help.
* *Insect bites, minor skin irritations:* A 1 percent topical hydrocortisone such as Cortaid is very helpful. Benadryl cream is especially effective for itchy bites.
* *Poison ivy and similar skin irritations:* Calamine lotion will reduce the itch and soothe the irritation.
* *Stuffy nose:* There are several available decongestants. (Before taking, check with your doctor if you have cardiac rhythm abnormality or high blood pressure.)
* *Mild cough:* I recommend preparations that contain dextromethorphan. The theobromine in dark chocolate may actually be as effective as most cough suppressants—and a lot more fun to take.
* *Allergy:* Use any of the over-the-counter antihistamines available. Look for one that doesn't leave you drowsy and remember that

they can all cause voiding problems in men with enlarged prostates. If you or any one in your family reacts badly to wasp or bee stings, you should have injectable epinephrine (Epipen) handy for emergencies.

* *Occasional constipation:* Try prune juice first. If that doesn't work, take a mild laxative such as Dulcolax, or a fiber-rich product such as FiberCon or Metamucil.

* *Minor cuts and scrapes:* Use an antibacterial ointment (most of them end with "sporin") such as Polysporin or Neosporin.

* *Minor burns:* Cold running water is much better than butter. Neosporin Plus prevents infection.

* *Poison:* In the event of acute poisoning, call the National Poison Control Center hotline anytime day or night at 1-800-222-1222 or 1-800-876-4766. Keep those numbers handy.

* *Acute nausea and vomiting:* I am partial to Compazine tablets or suppositories. (They require a prescription.)

These items are what you should have handy for some of the symptoms you may encounter in your everyday life. And remember that in every medicine or herb there is a little poison, whether or not it requires a prescription. Use the lowest dose of any medication for only as long as you absolutely need it. Unlike love or money, more is rarely better.

29

WINTERIZE YOUR HOME

DANNY LIPFORD

Danny Lipford is the host of the nationally syndicated television show, Today's Homeowner with Danny Lipford. *He also serves as the home improvement expert for* The Early Show *on CBS and the Weather Channel.*

Making your home more comfortable in winter is as simple as keeping the heated air in and the cold air out. Creating a tight seal or envelope around the living area of your home is crucial to driving down utility bills. Here's how to start:

TAKE A WALK

Walk around the perimeter of your home and carefully look for any crack or gap around windows, doors, dryer vents, outside faucets (hose bibs), or any place that might allow inside air out or outside air in. To fill cracks of three-eighths inch or less, a quality exterior caulk will do the job. If you want to paint over the caulk, an acrylic/latex caulk is your best bet. Larger gaps, like the ones where air-conditioner condenser lines exit the house, can be filled with expandable foam. Again, the latex variety is a good choice because it's easy to clean up.

CHECK YOUR ATTIC

Heat rises and will find a way to escape into your attic if you do not have a sufficient "blanket of insulation" above the living space. The amount of insulation you need will be determined by what part of the country you live in. Your local building inspection department can give you recommendations for the minimum insulation coverage in your area. If you have no attic insulation at all, consider hiring an insulation contractor to apply "blown-in" insulation. This is a relatively inexpensive and quick procedure. If you already have some insulation in your attic, consider adding unfaced fiberglass batts to make up any deficit. Unfaced insulation has no paper backing and can be rolled out over the top of your existing insulation.

WEATHER STRIPPING

Carefully inspect weather stripping around your doors and windows for any missing or damaged pieces. If your doors and windows are not sealed well, heated air will escape and cold air will get into the home. To check the quality of this seal, close the door and blow on it from the outside with a blow-dryer. Blow air around the perimeter while someone else holds a lighted candle on the interior, directly opposite the blow-dryer. If the flame flickers, the seal isn't tight enough.

There are many different types of weather stripping, so choose one that will attach well and provide the seal you need. If you are replacing damaged material, take a small piece with you to the home center to match it. The threshold, located on the floor under exterior doors, takes a lot of abuse and is important to maintaining a tight seal below the door. If you see significant wear and tear on the threshold, replace it.

FURNACE CHECKUPS

To ensure that your hardworking heating system is operating as efficiently as possible, commit to frequent furnace checkups. Hiring a professional heating contractor to clean and service your system at least twice a year is money well spent. Changing or cleaning your system's furnace filter is also important to its efficient operation and the health of your family. This should be done at two-to-three-month intervals.

UPGRADING YOUR WINDOWS

Old or low-quality single-pane windows can allow the cold air outside to drastically influence the interior temperatures, which forces the heating system to work harder. Replacement windows are a fairly inexpensive option to solve this problem. The old windows are removed by collapsing them within the framework of the opening without affecting the exterior or interior walls or trim. Custom-sized windows are made, installed, and secured in the opening using screws to connect to the home's framing. This approach saves tons of money on reframing, retrimming, and painting. These windows generally have solid vinyl frames that include a thermal break that prevents cold temperatures from transferring to the inside.

According to the Department of Energy, the average cost to heat a home is approximately $1,400 a year. By making the kinds of changes outlined above, you may be able to cut this amount in half.

30

CONTROL MOLD

JEFFREY C. MAY

Jeffrey C. May is founder and principal of May Indoor Air Investigations LLC in Cambridge, Massachusetts. He is the author of My House is Killing Me! The Home Guide for Families with Allergies and Asthma *and co-author of* The Mold Survival Guide: For Your Home and for Your Health.

Is your unfinished basement musty? Are there black spots on your bathroom ceiling? Perhaps you accepted an offer for your house, the home inspector found mold in your attic, and the buyer withdrew. Or the seller of your new house said the finished basement was dry, and then you found mold growing behind the paneling. Mold can be a health, legal, and financial problem that has cost the insurance industry billions of dollars.

Do not accept the premise that mold is everywhere and, therefore, not a concern. While it is true that mold spores are in the air we breath and the dust around us, these seeds only germinate and colonize surfaces when conditions are conducive to their growth. Fungi (mold/mildew) grow at indoor temperatures, need a food source (paper, wood, dust, leather, cotton, and even soap scum), and require oxygen from the air, but moisture is the limiting, most essential component for growth. This moisture can be due to liquid water from leaks or vapor in air from high relative humidity. Since some mildew fungi can grow in 75 percent relative humidity (RH), controlling the amount of water vapor in the air is the best way to control mold growth.

Where can mold grow in your home?

* In a crawl space, basement, and bathroom and, in cold climates, in closets at exterior walls, and in the attic
* On dust in a carpet laid on a cool surface (like concrete on soil) or in a carpet that is frequently damp
* On the dust in a heat pump, window air conditioner, baseboard convector, radiator, furnace, and ducts and even on the dust in an exposed basement or crawl-space fiberglass insulation
* On furniture stored in damp spaces

Here are some practical steps you can take to keep mold at bay:

* Buy a digital hygrometer to measure RH; then use a *dehumidifier* in the summer to keep the RH below 50 percent in your basement (and keep the basement windows closed when the dehumidifier is running).
* If you use a *humidifier* in the winter, don't let the RH go much above 30 percent. A warm-mist portable humidifier is preferable to a cool-mist one.
* Keep a finished basement or "cold" closet consistently warm (not under 60°F) in the winter.
* After showering, operate the bathroom exhaust, keep the shower enclosure and bathroom door open, and run a tabletop, oscillating fan to speed the drying of surfaces.

* To avoid dust accumulations, any heating or cooling system (including a window air conditioner) should have a filter with at least a MERV 6 rating.
* Have ducts and cooling coils professionally cleaned.
* Clean all dust from baseboard convectors and radiators.
* Use only a HEPA-filtered vacuum for all cleaning.
* Do not install carpeting below grade, at an entranceway, or in a bathroom or kitchen.
* If you remove a musty carpet, don't forget to get rid of the stair and hallway runners.
* Don't store furniture in a damp basement or garage.
* Before bringing them into your home, check the bottoms and backs of all antiques for mold.
* Never vent a bathroom or dryer exhaust indoors or into an attic or crawl space.
* If you have excessive condensation on windows, install a stove exhaust fan, vent it to the outside, and use it when you cook.

Don't be casual about mold growth. If you find it in your home, figure out why it's there and seek professional guidance as you research safe and effective remedies.

31

CARE FOR YOUR CLOTHING

STEVE BOORSTEIN

Steve Boorstein, aka The Clothing Doctor, is a clothier, dry cleaner extraordinaire, and fabric expert. He is executive director of Leading Cleaners Internationale and the author of The Ultimate Guide to Shopping and Caring for Clothing.

CARING FOR BETTER CLOTHING (NONWASHABLES)

The care of clothing starts the moment you begin shopping. Before reaching the cash register, inspect the garment up and down, spin it around and check the zippers, hooks, hems, seams, snags, stains, and buttons. Always ask for extra buttons!

* Hair spray, perfume, cologne, and deodorant cause many seemingly harmless and invisible stains that surface *after* dry cleaning! Apply them before you dress and let them dry completely.
* Most mistakes are made in the first 10 seconds, so in a "stain emergency," count to ten, relax, gently *blot* the stained area with a dry, white napkin, and *stop*. Never rub a fabric.
* Think of water and club soda as the same. Use them sparingly and do *not* apply to oily stains such as French fries, gravy,

dressing, or lipstick. They can spread stains, bleed dyes, and form rings, often making removal by your dry cleaner an impossible task.

* Dry cleaning should be your first choice for oily stains.
* Air out all clothing for an hour after wearing and inspect under bright light before rehanging.
* Dry clean or wash all stained clothing within 24 to 48 hours.

While many store-bought and home remedies work safely on washable clothing, please do not confuse the message: most remedies should not be used on dry-clean-only clothing or certain fabrics or colors. Instead, leave the stain removal to skilled technicians, and stop looking for quick fixes and miracle cures.

CLOSET CARE

* Remove all dry-cleaning plastic. Keep the paper shoulder covers on clothing to protect from dust and fading.
* Use plastic and wooden hangers whenever possible and stay away from skirt clip hangers with "teeth." No wire hangers!
* Each time you buy a new garment, edit your wardrobe by discarding or donating an old garment.

TRAVEL

Many garments are damaged while traveling, so pay attention!

* Seal all hair spray and liquids in a double Ziploc bag. They can leak and explode under pressure and *cannot* be removed from clothing.
* To find a good dry cleaner when traveling, call the ritziest clothing store in town and ask the manager which cleaner they use.
* Pack in a hurry and throw it all in, if you must, but *never* leave home without the best-kept secret in clothing care—a travel steamer!

DRY CLEANERS

Good clothing deserves exceptional care.

* Choose a dry cleaner for quality, service, convenience, and price—in that order.
* Show your dry cleaner fabric pills, snags, and pressing problems. Give them permission to do minor repairs up to $15 without calling.
* Point out stains (even personal ones) and identify the source. Don't be shy because dry cleaners have seen it all before!
* If a garment's been lost by your dry cleaner, allow 3 weeks for it to be returned or replaced.
* If your dry cleaner admits to damaging your garment and it cannot be repaired to your satisfaction, you're entitled to a "like" replacement or a cash settlement within 1 week.

STORING CLOTHING

* Dry clean or wash all *worn* and stained clothing before storing (even if the garment has been worn for only 5 minutes).
* Insects are attracted to moisture, food particles, perspiration, body oil, cologne, and perfume.
* When storing clothing at home, keep garments out of basements and attics. Cover hanging items with a freshly washed, unbleached cotton sheet.
* When storing clothing with your dry cleaner, make a computerized list and give the dry cleaner a copy to compare inventories.

32

PROTECT YOUR KIDS ONLINE

PARRY AFTAB

Parry Aftab is a cyber-lawyer. She is an advocate for Internet

safety for children and victims of cyber-stalking. She is the

author of The Parent's Guide to Protecting Your Children

in Cyberspace *and executive director of* Wired Safety,

the world's largest Internet safety and help group.

Every day hundreds of parents ask me how to protect their kids online. Questions range from "Should I even let them use the Internet?" to "How can I supervise them when I don't know how to turn on the computer?"

First, don't panic.

Second, know that the greatest single risk our children face in connection with the Internet is being denied access. I have a solution for everything else.

Third, you won't be able to scrutinize everything they do, control every place they visit, or screen everyone they communicate with online. While you might be able to do that for kids under the age of eight, it no longer works when the kids become preteens. By then, you have to rely on the filter between their ears.

While parents often ask about the latest software to block and filter sites (check out wiredkids.org), block annoying communications (instant-messaging security settings), or check on what your children are doing and who they are talking to online (spectorsoft.com), and while they worry about cracking the chat lingo code (teenangels.org's chat translator) to learn their children's secrets, they are missing the point. It's not about technology at all. It's about parenting.

Everything you need to know about keeping your children safe online you learned from your parents, and they learned from theirs. While you may need me to point out the latest abuses and tricks of the trade, the basics remain unchanged.

"Come straight home after school." This kept us from hanging around with the wrong crowd and getting into trouble. It's no different online. The longer the kids spend online (other than for homework purposes), the more likely they are to engage in high-risk activities, such as sharing personal information, meeting strangers offline, and engaging in cybersex.

"Don't take candy from strangers." You never know what that candy could be laced with. And when you accept anything from strangers online, it may include spyware, hacking programs, and viruses.

"Don't get into a car with strangers." Or meet them offline (at least not without you in attendance). A stranger is a stranger, but when our kids chat with them for a week, or longer, they don't feel like a stranger anymore. That's where the real dangers arise.

"Do unto others the way you would have them do unto you." Adapted for cyberspace, it means never to do anything online that you wouldn't do offline, and never say anything online that you wouldn't say to the person face-to-face.

"Don't take anything that isn't yours." I know that having our kids download music for free is tempting. But it's still stealing. It shouldn't make any difference that other kids are doing it. (Remember the old parental standby: "I don't care what your friends are doing.")

If you teach them these things, you don't have to learn about the latest technologies. The list of those is extensive and changes constantly anyway. If you teach them to come to you when things go wrong online and off, and if you promise not to overreact if they do, they'll make it through this in one piece and so will you. I promise.

Heck, contrary to my mother's prediction, I survived the Beatles.

33

PLAN FOR RETIREMENT

RIC EDELMAN

Ric Edelman is the author of five books on personal finance,

including the recently released third edition of his national best-

seller, The Truth About Money. *His firm, Edelman Financial*

Services LLC, manages more than $2.4 billion in client assets.

Edelman also writes a nationally syndicated financial advice

column for United Media and hosts weekly radio and

television shows in the Washington, D.C., area.

Retirement. You spend years dreaming about it (and maybe even saving for it). Still, many people worry about having enough money to retire comfortably.

Whether you're planning to leave work altogether, planning to work part time, or thinking about starting a second career, the decision to retire is a big step, and it can be made much easier with proper planning. The following steps can help you get started now.

1. HOW MUCH INCOME WILL YOU NEED ANNUALLY?
Chances are you'll spend as much money in retirement as you do now, maybe more. So start by making a list of all your current

annual expenses that you are likely to incur after you retire. Consider your family obligations when listing these expenditures. Preparing for retirement can be easy—if you don't have to worry about paying for college, weddings, or caring for elderly parents at the same time. Too often, people focus on one aspect of their financial lives without considering the rest of their situation. That's a recipe for trouble.

2. DETERMINE YOUR SOURCES OF INCOME

You are likely to have several sources of income after you retire: Social Security, a pension, your portfolio, and income from employment. Most retirees receive a monthly Social Security check. Check your most recent copy of your Social Security statement, sent to you once a year about ninety days before your birthday (or you can request a current statement by going to www.ssa.gov). The statement projects your monthly Social Security check using today's dollars for three ages: sixty-two, sixty-five, and seventy.

Many retirees also receive income from a company pension or retirement plan. You should also be putting money into savings and investments accounts—and if you haven't, start now!

If you plan to retire in a few years, yet have not been adequately funding your retirement, you may need to work part time after your career ends.

3. ADJUST ALL THE ABOVE NUMBERS FOR INFLATION AND TAXES

Over the past twenty years, inflation has averaged 4.5 percent per year. This means a person who retired in 1985 on a fixed income has 59 percent less to live on today than when he first retired. Also, be aware that most, perhaps all, of your income in retirement will be taxable—just like it is today. Make sure you'll be able to afford retirement after revising your numbers to reflect inflation and taxes. So get out your calculator and adjust your numbers.

4. COMPARE YOUR EXPENDITURES WITH YOUR INCOME

After updating these numbers, subtract your total retirement expenditures from your total sources of income. Chances are you will discover that your retirement is underfunded. To fund your shortfall, you probably should be contributing significantly more than you currently are to your retirement plan at work (such as a 401(k), 403(b), or 457 plan). After maximizing your contributions to your retirement plan, see if you are eligible to contribute to an IRA. If so, contribute the maximum. If you are not eligible, start to invest in variable annuities.

OTHER THINGS YOU NEED TO CONSIDER

Protecting your assets from taxes and probate requires your attention now. For many people, a sound estate plan includes a will, trusts, a medical directive, and powers of attorney. Get these documents drafted or updated by hiring a lawyer who specializes in wills and trusts.

Prior to celebrating your fiftieth birthday, you should consider purchasing a long-term care policy. You'll want to sign up for Medicare parts A and B three months prior to turning age sixty-five; you also should consider purchasing Medigap insurance at that time.

Adequately preparing for retirement is not a do-it-yourself activity. Although you can do some of this preparation work on your own, I recommend seeking the help of a financial advisor. Professional guidance can be invaluable in reviewing the structure of your portfolio, making sure you are adequately diversified, knowing how to best fund your retirement, and determining your best options and strategies in preparing for retirement.

34

CLEAN YOUR POOL OR SPA

TERRY TAMMINEN

As the "Malibu pool man to the stars," Terry Tamminen's client list included Dustin Hoffman, Barbra Streisand, and Sting. He is the best-selling author of three pool books, including The Ultimate Pool Maintenance Manual. *Active in protecting coastal waters, Tamminen was tapped by Governor Arnold Schwarzenegger to be secretary of the California Environmental Protection Agency. He now serves as Cabinet Secretary for the state of California.*

There's a Zen quality to the otherwise mundane task of cleaning your pool or spa. That's because nothing is more soothing than being in and around water.

Here's how the pros do it.

1. CLEAN THE DECK AND COVER. A quick sweep of the pool/spa deck and cover will keep the water clean after you leave.

2. ADJUST THE WATER LEVEL. Check the water level—it may take some time to make up for any evaporation, so put the hose into the pool/spa immediately.

3. SKIM THE SURFACE. Using your leaf rake, or "telepole" (a telescoping pole with a mesh bag at one end), work your way around the pool/spa and rake debris off the surface. Scrape the tile line as you skim to get dirt off the tiles. *Hint:* squirt a small amount of tile soap over the width of the water to spread debris toward the edges of the pool/spa.

4. CLEAN THE TILES. Apply tile soap to a pool/spa tile brush (or a barbecue cleaning pad) and start scrubbing. Scrub both above and below the waterline. *Hint:* don't use kitchen soaps, as they will create suds. Do use a foam knee pad!

5. CHECK THE EQUIPMENT. Clean out the skimmer basket at the water's edge and empty debris from the strainer basket on the pump. *Hint:* clean up the equipment area. Leaves around motor vents or the heater could cause fires; clear deck drains of debris that could cause floods during rain.

6. VACUUM. Attach your pool vacuum head to the telepole and attach the vacuum hose to the vacuum head. Feed the vacuum head straight down into the water with the hose following, so water fills the hose and displaces all of the air. Slide the other end of the hose through the skimmer opening, attaching it to the skimmer's suction port. Vacuuming a pool/spa is no different from vacuuming your carpet—work your way around the bottom and sides of the pool/spa. *Hint:* avoid moving the vacuum head too quickly or you will stir up the dirt! When finished, remove your vacuum and check the pump strainer basket to see if it has clogged with debris from vacuuming. Clean as needed.

7. MONITOR CHEMICALS. Use a chlorine (or other sanitizer) and pH test kit. Follow the instructions to determine how much product you

need to add and apply the chemicals based on the volume of your pool/spa. *Hint:* walk around your pool/spa as you apply chemicals for even distribution.

8. BRUSH THE POOL/SPA. Attach a brush to your telepole and brush the sides and bottom of the pool/spa to remove any stains or stubborn dirt. Brush toward the main drain so that dirt is sucked out of the pool/spa.

9. CLEAN UP/CLOSE UP. Clean up your equipment and supplies and take one last look to make sure you added enough water, turned off the water supply, and picked up everything you brought with you.

Now jump in and enjoy the fruits of your labor!

BE SAFE IN THE SUN

Fredric Brandt

Dr. Fredric Brandt has been practicing dermatology for more

than twenty years. He is the creator of Dr. Brandt Skincare,

a line of skin and sun protection products, and the author

of Age-less: The Definitive Guide to Botox, Peels,

Collagen & Other Solutions for Flawless Skin.

We all love our sun. Yet the energy emitted from the sun's surface can damage our skin. One of the atmosphere's functions is to filter harmful rays coming in from the sun and from space and prevent them from hitting the surface of the earth. In the past two decades, however, the atmosphere has been thinning thanks to environmental and industrial pollution, leaving all living organisms on the surface of the earth increasingly exposed to harmful cosmic radiation.

The sun emits an array of high- and low-frequency radiation of which ultraviolet (UV) light is the most dangerous for our skin. UV light cannot be seen by the naked eye and exists in two different forms: UVA and UVB. UVA has the longer wave length, so it can penetrate the skin to deeper parts; and UVB has the shorter one, which is absorbed closer to the surface. These rays can lead to numerous problems ranging from accelerated skin aging and wrinkles to skin cancer.

When we are exposed to the sun, our skin initially tries to fight off the aggressive UV rays. However, if the defense mechanisms get overwhelmed, damage will occur to vital parts of our skin. This damage leads to inflammation and is manifested as a sunburn with red, itchy skin. It can have serious consequences, even years later. The most feared problem is skin cancer, which can be dangerous and requires the attention of a dermatologist. Other consequences can be permanent freckles and brown spots on your skin and the premature development of wrinkles.

To avoid all this, we need to protect our skin from the sun on a daily basis. Here are some important tips:

1. AVOID THE SUN. Don't sun tan and please stay away from tanning beds, which can be worse than the sun. Try to avoid going outside during the peak hours of 11 A.M. to 4 P.M., when the sun is the strongest. If you need to go outside, as most people do, wear appropriate protective clothing and cover any exposed area of your skin. Hats are very important, and wide brims are best.

2. APPLY SUNSCREEN. This should become part of your daily morning routine. Apply sunscreen to exposed face, neck, hands, arms, legs, and feet. This is the most effective measure you can take to prevent sun damage, and it should be done even if you are not planning to lay out. Regardless of climate or temperature, the UV rays will penetrate through clouds and even through our clothes. Use a sunscreen with a minimum sun protection factor (SPF) of 15 or higher. Sunscreen with an SPF of 30 or higher offers you maximum protection from the sun, blocking out 96 percent of UV light. Sunscreen

with an SPF of 15 or higher will block out 93 percent. Apply sufficient amounts to cover the skin evenly, ideally 30 minutes before you go outside. If you are doing outdoor activities, use a waterproof sunscreen and reapply it every 2 hours to preserve its effect. Never use sunscreen to extend the amount of time you would normally spend in the sun.

3. DON'T FORGET YOUR SUNGLASSES. Like your skin, your eyes are at risk if exposed to excessive UV radiation. When buying sunglasses, you can gauge their effectiveness by checking the swing tag on the sunglasses to ensure lenses block out 95 percent of UV. Polarizing lenses reduce glare substantially and are favored by many people for comfort, but polarization itself has little effect on the UV-absorbing properties of lenses. Similarly, mirror finishes by themselves do not significantly reduce UV absorption.

There is no such thing as a "safe tan," and sun exposure should be avoided at all costs. Protecting your skin from an early age will prevent problems in the future and will keep you looking young.

TO IMPROVE

36

MAKE THE MOST OF A SPARE ROOM

SUSIE COELHO

Designer Susie Coelho is a lifestyle expert and the bestselling author of two books, Everyday Styling *and* Styling for Entertainment. *She has hosted two series on HGTV,* Surprise Gardener *and* Outer Spaces, *and designs a line of bedding, bath, and tabletop décor.*

Spare room. The phrase conjures up a fairy-tale image of a lonely princess knocking around a drafty castle. In this day and age, the term sounds more like an oxymoron—how can a whole room be spare?

Occasionally, however, you end up with one. Let's hope it's because your career is booming and you move into an apartment or house that's bigger than you need. Or maybe one of your kids finally leaves the nest, abandoning a bedroom. I came by mine when I got divorced. (Caution: this technique only works if your ex had a home office or a den.)

Spare rooms are dangerous, especially when bored, and they

bore easily. Leave one empty and it will fill itself. I made the mistake of trying to keep my newly spare room empty while I figured out the best use for it. I put in only a desk and a computer, thinking it would make a great indoor home office, even though I already had a home studio in my converted garage. Soon my fourteen-year-old moved in his boom box and started reconfiguring my files. My four-year-old daughter followed suit by dragging in her drawing table, taping original art to my freshly painted walls, and finger-painting next to my rugs.

Thus did I learn the first secret of taming a spare room: don't let the bored creature amuse itself by biting off chunks from other parts of the house. Instead of using more space for the same old stuff, figure out how the extra space can expand your life—the art you keep talking about doing, the sculpting, the writing. How about a sewing room, a library, a place to display your collections, a home office, a playroom, or even a classroom? If the whole family is into hobbies and crafts, you can create a shared workroom. For a family studio, buy an armoire, entertainment center, or office wall unit to house the equipment and supplies, all behind doors or in drawers.

Often, though, the activity you have in mind doesn't require a whole room. A writer only needs a desk and a bookshelf; a seamstress needs only enough space for a sewing machine, mannequin, and table. With the rest of the spare room at loose ends, the bored monster starts looking for mischief. Which brings us to the second secret of taming the spare room: multitasking.

A spare room enables you to enhance your home in several ways at once. A simple sofa bed lets the new home office double as a guestroom. Throw in a treadmill or an exercise bike, and it's your gym, too. If you still have space, a flat-screen TV and a stereo will give the kids a place to entertain when you want the living room for yourself.

Consider the activities that would make life better for you and your family and how your spare room can help make them an integral part of your home. Finally, think about how you can fit them together in the same space.

The most fun about a spare room? Setting it up in the first place. Treat it as a blank canvas, an uncut block of marble, a new page.

37

ORGANIZE YOUR CLOSET

Anthony Vidergauz

Anthony Vidergauz is the president and CEO of California Closet Company, Inc., the fastest-growing and most profitable franchise in the installed closet industry with over 156 locations worldwide.

Organization is both an art and a science. The art is in creating a space that allows you to feel at ease within it as well as a haven to store all of the things that are meaningful to you. The science of organization is in knowing how to bring the art to life.

Here are several secrets to designing an organized closet that will provide you with a space you are proud to show off and be within.

1. GROUP SIMILAR ITEMS TOGETHER. Instead of mixing items through your closet, keep areas designated for specific items, such as suits, shirts, and casual clothes. This will make it easier to find them.

2. TRY NOT TO USE THE FLOOR FOR STORAGE. This is an area that is typically without light, and when you have clothes hanging

over the space, it makes it very difficult to see what is stored below. Instead, make the best use of space with stacking bins or additional storage shelves above your hanging pole.

3. UTILIZE THE SPACE OF OPEN WALLS. Adding hooks or belt and tie racks on small side walls within your closet will maximize the usable space and will provide you with a specific area for small items.

4. DESIGNATE AREAS FOR SHOE STORAGE. Shoes are often the most disorganized items within a closet. Built-in shoe cubbies, stacking shoe organizer boxes, or even shoe boxes will allow you to easily establish what shoes you have and will also keep them in good condition when they are not being worn.

5. KEEP YOUR SWEATERS LOOKING THEIR BEST. Instead of hanging your sweaters, or stuffing them inside a drawer, carefully fold them on shelves. In stacks of three to four each, you will have greater visibility into what you have, and they will not get stretched out while they are being stored.

6. CREATE THE ILLUSION OF MORE SPACE. When organizing your closet, do not overfill the space just as you walk in. This will give you the sense of being crowded, and it will appear even more disorganized. Instead, use this area for smaller items, such as stacked shoe boxes, or shelving. If you have two levels of hanging within your closet, utilize the upper section for items that are not as bulky, like folded pants and casual tops, and utilize the lower hanging section for bulkier items, such as jackets, long-sleeved shirts, and suits. By taking the bulk out of the higher level, you will provide the illusion and feeling of more space as you move through your closet and provide youself with greater visibility of your entire wardrobe without being blocked by bulky clothes.

7. DESIGNATE AREAS FOR MEMORABILIA. Beautiful boxes can be purchased to store family heirlooms, wedding dresses, old photographs, and love letters. Place a note card on the side of the box that indicates what is stored within. These can then be stacked on the top shelf of your closet and easily identified when you wish to sort through them.

Once you have organized your space, it will be much easier to maintain.

38

CLEAN A CARPET

CARL F. WILLIAMS

Carl F. Williams refers to himself as an overeducated janitor.
He is past president of the Carpet Cleaner's Institute (CCI)
and has been awarded CCI's Joe Laurino Carpet Cleaner of
the Year award. He is the author of countless books and
articles on carpet cleaning and floor coverings.

If you don't make cleaning fun, you're about to have a back-breaking, miserable time. If you involve friends and family in the process, it's a hoot.

PREPARATION

Vacuum the carpeting thoroughly to avoid making mud pies. Next, find the adjustment for the hot-water heater and turn it up. Avoid staining curtains by hanging the bottom third over a coat hanger and hooking them on the rod.

Wash your hands before smearing grease on the upholstered furniture as you move it. Never move the furniture more than its width. When lifting, use your legs, not your back. Now vacuum behind the furniture.

Next, grab aluminum foil and scissors and cut up 4-inch

squares to be used under the furniture to protect the carpet against furniture stain or metal rust. Leave the furniture out from the wall until after you've cleaned the carpet.

THE MACHINE

Have a cleaner reserved so you don't have to drive around town looking for one on the day of cleaning. Carpet is easier to clean without a hurry-up mentality. Make sure that the machine is free of dirty water. Turn it on and see if it sprays clear water.

You will be cleaning from the farthest point in the house from the front door. Standard extraction cleaning equipment comes with two 10-gallon tanks, one for the cleaning solution and the other for the extracted dirty water. This dirty water has to be emptied as often as fresh cleaning solution is added.

Begin by setting up your machine and stretching the hoses and wand to the farthermost point. Set up your filling station in the bathroom where you will use a bathtub to fill a 2-gallon bucket with water for the machine and a toilet to empty the dirty water. All mixing is done in the bathroom on an old towel. Never use the same bucket to fill clean water and empty dirty water because the organic load will reduce the effectiveness of the cleaning solution. Use a separate 5-gallon bucket to remove the old dirty water from the machine.

CLEANING

Now start your cleaning stroke by spraying solution in a straight line using one stroke with the detergent spray and two strokes to dry the carpeting. The forward and backward motion should travel about 30 inches, depending on your height. You are now starting to paint your way (so to speak) out of the house. The carpet will begin to look beautiful. When finished, place aluminum foil squares under the table legs as you slide the furniture back into place.

When it comes time to empty and refill the machine, be careful not to leave any water in either of the buckets because a small child could tip into either one without a sound.

DRYING

After you've finished the carpet cleaning, use a box-type fan to accelerate the drying. The blowing will turn the remaining liquid moisture on the carpet into a vapor. The humidity level will get really high almost immediately. Most folks think that the fastest way to dry a carpet is to turn the heat up—wrong. Mold grows actively between 68 and 86 degrees Fahrenheit, so by increasing the heat you start growing a fungus. Instead, turn the air conditioner on and set it at 68 degrees Fahrenheit to reduce the humidity. The room will dry completely within 2 to 8 hours.

THE FINISH

Clean up the machine by vacuuming any remaining water out of the cleaning solution tank, emptying the dirty water, and cleaning the machine before you return it.

When you return home, stay off the carpet to let it dry. Look around and smile because you have saved hundreds of dollars by doing the job yourself.

39

UNCLOG A TOILET

RAYMOND P. VINZANT

Raymond P. VinZant is the Roto-Rooter Ask-the-Plumber

Answer Man and teaches plumbing at Anoka Technical

College. He has been appointed to the Higher Education

Facilities Board for Minnesota.

Just when you thought everything was okay, you see your three-year-old walking proudly out of the bathroom. You realize Bobo, his blue toy tugboat, is not permanently glued to his hand—and you hear the toilet filling, but you didn't hear that swoosh of a flush. You rush into the bathroom, as the slurry in the toilet bowl is less than an inch from the top. But you keep your cool, reach under the left side of the tank and shut off the water, at the little chrome valve alongside the toilet. You knew right where it was . . . and you knew if you turned off the source, the bowl would immediately quit filling.

But now what do you do? The toilet is filled with a roll of toilet paper, a special little log is lingering, and Bobo has been torpedoed.

The first step is to lower the water level in the toilet bowl so there won't be a mess. This is done by donning a set of latex gloves and dipping the water into a bucket with a plastic throw-away cup. Once the water is at its normal level, you can begin to work on the toilet. The bucket can be cleaned with a little bleach and waste-water poured back into the toilet after you're done.

AUGERS

A toilet auger can be purchased at any hardware store and is a must for the emergency home-plumbing kit. It can save you a 10-minute plumbing call costing you professional rates. The auger is inserted into the toilet bowl with the cable fully retracted into its protective shaft. Any exposed cable can leave ugly black scratch marks on the white ceramic at the bottom of the toilet.

Crank the cable clockwise applying downward pressure on the handle, to screw it into the trap. The spring on the end of the auger should snag the object or break up any paper clog. When you hook the toy, the snake will become difficult to turn. At this point, try to pull the toy back through the trap. Do not crank the snake backward or you will lose it. Pull the snake back into the  sheath of the auger and, with any luck, you will retrieve the object. You may have to do this a few times before you actually extract the obstruction.

PLUNGERS

Though plungers do not work for retrieving an item that has lodged itself into the toilet, for most clogs a plunger is a first-step solution. As you put the plunger into the filled bowl, turn it on a diagonal, so the air can flow out of the rubber bell. When you push down on the

plunger, use strokes that will create force inside the trap but will not splash water out of the toilet, especially if the toilet is still full of slushy excrement. Start slowly with the stroke and if you can't clear the toilet without splashing, try reversing the pull. Slowly push the plunger down over the opening, then pull back fast, creating a negative pressure in the trap of the toilet. If you can't clear the toilet this way, you will have to try an auger.

DRAIN CLEANERS

Contrary to popular belief, acid drain cleaners like Drano are not quick toilet-clog fixes. Though they are designed to work against hair and grease buildup in small pipes, they typically fail miserably in larger pipes, like the one under a toilet. Because they are acidic, these drain cleaners can eat holes through steel piping. Plumbers regularly encounter piping broken down in older homes by repeated use of acid drain cleaners. This is hazardous not only to the piping but to the plumber who has to work on the pipe when the cleaner fails to unclog the toilet. When acid-based drain cleaners leak through the holes they have caused in the piping, they can contaminate the groundwater and pollute the environment.

DISCONNECTING THE TOILET

If you have exhausted your options and you absolutely cannot dislodge the blockage, call a plumber; or if you're handy, pull up the toilet and attack the problem from the backside. Disconnecting the toilet isn't as difficult as it sounds. The first step is to remove the water from the toilet. I use a wet vac. Then unscrew the supply tube from the bottom of the tank. Remove the white caps and the nuts on the flange on each side of the toilet. Then rock the toilet side to side, lift it gently off the floor, and set it upside down on a large piece of cardboard. You can then use the auger to push the object backward through the trap. Typically you cannot remove it through the opening on the bottom, because it is smaller than the trap. Clean off the old seal and reset the toilet with a *new* wax ring, closet bolts, and supply tube. Always follow the instructions with the new parts. Finally, turn on the water, test the toilet, sit back, and enjoy your accomplishment.

40

FIX A FAUCET

Ed Del Grande

Ed Del Grande holds three active master licenses in plumbing,

pipefitting, and fire protection. He hosts DIY's Ed the Plumber

and writes a nationally syndicated newspaper column

distributed by Scripps/Howard News Service.

Let's start with a simple faucet repair that you can make without even replacing parts: a slow-running faucet, one of the most common problems. If you notice that your faucet runs slowly when both the hot and cold water are turned on, chances are you have a partially blocked aerator. The aerator is located at the end of your faucet and it softens the flow of water by introducing air into the flow. It also has a screen or restrictor built in to the top that can clog up with debris from your system. To fix it, simply unscrew the aerator from the spout, clean off the debris with an old toothbrush, and reinstall the aerator, making sure the washer is seated properly.

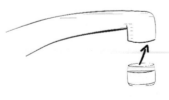

In anticipation of other problems, a good do-it-yourself

plumber needs to know the different makes and models of faucets before starting the repairs. When purchasing a new faucet, keep all the factory papers with the make and model number. If you don't have any paperwork for your current faucets, you can do some homework to find out the make and model to prepare for what might arise.

BATHROOM SINKS

Bathroom faucets, also known as lav faucets, come in 4-inch or 8-inch models. To find the size of your lav faucet, measure the spread from the center of the hot-water handle to the center of the cold-water handle. Four-inch models are usually a deck-mount style, which means the body is all one piece and simply sits on the deck of the lav sink as one unit. Handle designs on a 4-inch model can be either a two-handle setup or they can have one handle in the center. Eight-inch models are usually separate components that are installed in each hole of the lav sink and in most cases will be a two-handle design with a separate spout in the middle.

UTILITY SINKS

Faucets on bar sinks or laundry sinks fall into the utility faucet category. Even though there are many styles of utility faucets and the spouts will be extra high or extra long, the main workings of the utility faucet will be similar to a 4-inch deck-mounted lav faucet and, in most cases, can be repaired just like its lav faucet counterpart.

KITCHEN SINKS

Kitchen faucets have the widest array of features. Not only are you dealing with different faucet styles with hot- and cold-water valves, but they will usually have spray heads with diverter valves built into them. Models range from a one-handle to a two-handle operation, high spout, short spout, pull-out spray head, remote spray head, deck mounted, and component mounted. Most kitchen faucets have a remote spray head, and that is the source of most problems. Some common spray head problems and solutions include:

* When the spray head is turned on, no water comes on or you get very low spray head pressure combined with water still emerging from faucet. This is usually caused by a bad diverter valve inside the faucet body. To correct it, you will need to get a replacement diverter kit.
* The spray head handle breaks off or the head cracks and leaks. This problem is common because the head itself is plastic. You can replace a spray head in a snap with very little money.

A good spray head maintenance tip is to soak your spray head in white vinegar to dissolve minerals and keep it looking new. Shiny faucets will make your entire kitchen look cleaner.

When it comes time for a faucet repair, you can now go to your local home center with all your information and the symptoms of your broken faucet. Information is the best tool in your box! Armed with your make and model information, you can get the exact factory repair parts you'll need with complete instructions on how to make the specific repair. No matter how prepared you are, keep in mind that in some situations, replacing the old faucet may be your best option.

And remember, there are plumbers who know how to deal with just about any plumbing emergency and they are always there to back you up if you ever get in way over your head!

41

SELECT AND CLEAN COUNTERTOPS

TERRI MCGRAW

Terri McGraw, aka Mrs. Fixit, is the author of

Pantry Power *and* Mrs. Fixit Easy Home Repair.

Her syndicated home improvement segments and hints

appear on TV stations nationwide.

Your household countertops are some of the most used surfaces in your home. When selecting countertops, consider your lifestyle and the maintenance involved to make the counters last. There are four general categories: laminate, tile, solid surface, and natural stone. Here are some pros, cons, and care of each:

1. LAMINATE

This is the most common and one of the least expensive types of countertops. It is easy to work with, and it comes in a wide variety of colors and styles. On the downside, laminate countertops are susceptible to burns, stains, and chipping, and they cannot be repaired once damaged. They are easy to care for as long as you avoid abrasive cleansers or scrubbers. For everyday cleaning use soap and water. For stain removal, use a spray bottle filled with rubbing alcohol, which also doubles as a disinfectant. Another easy stain remover is lemon juice, rubbed directly into stains or scrubbed into the area with a cut lemon. Before removing stains from laminate, test any cleaning solution on a hidden area to be sure it won't result in discoloring.

2. CERAMIC TILE

Less expensive and more versatile, durable, and heat resistant than laminate, ceramic tile comes in many colors and styles. Care and cleaning of ceramic tile are similar to laminate; warm soapy water every day will take care of it. To make your own heavy-duty tile cleaner, mix 1 teaspoon borax, 1 teaspoon baking soda, 2 teaspoons lemon juice, ¼ teaspoon dish soap, and 2 cups hot water in a spray bottle. This concoction is a great solution for cleaning both grout and tile; just make sure that you label the bottle clearly! If you have stubborn spots, grab a pair of rubber gloves and make a paste of baking soda and laundry bleach. Dip an old toothbrush into the mixture and scrub away the stains.

3. SOLID SURFACE

These counters are extremely durable and have no seams. They are heat and water resistant, and scratches can be sanded out. For all that durability you will pay more, but it is an investment that usually pays for itself when you sell your home. When it comes to care, the procedure will change depending upon the type of solid surface that you choose (matte/satin, semi-gloss, and high gloss). Matte/satin finish is the most common solid countertop and can be cleaned with vinegar and water from a spray bottle. For stubborn stains, use a powdered cleanser and a green scrubber pad. A semi-gloss surface is slightly more delicate; treat stains with baking soda or a nonabrasive bleach-based cleanser and a white scrubber pad, which is less abrasive than a green pad. A high-gloss surface should be treated with an even gentler hand, so use the same nonabrasive cleanser, but choose a sponge instead of a scrubber pad.

4. STONE

For about the same cost as a solid surface you can choose beautiful slab stone countertops. Some common choices are granite, marble, soapstone, limestone, or aggregate. They are virtually indestructible. However, stone is a porous, natural mineral so it may react with common household products like juices, shaving cream, alcohol, perfumes, mustard, and common chemical cleansers. To minimize risk of staining and damage, stone countertops should be treated every six months with a sealant that will saturate the stone and protect it from common elements. There is no way to remove a stain from a porous stone, but you can push it farther into the stone so it's not as noticeable. To do this, spread hydrogen peroxide over the stain and leave it for several hours. If you don't have any hydrogen peroxide, try some baking soda and warm water. There are also specialty-cleaning solutions available for shining and polishing stone countertops.

42

HANG SHELVES

Lynda Lyday

Lynda Lyday is a professional carpenter and host of
TALK2DIY Home Improvement. *She is the author of* Lynda
Lyday's Do-It-Yourself! The Illustrated, Step-by-Step Guide
to the Most Popular Home Renovation and Repair Projects.
She recently released her own line of tools.

I f you fret over hanging a shelf on your own, you are not alone, but here's the good news: it's quite simple as long as you know a few basic tips.

THE WALL

A quick way to find out what your walls are made of is to put your hand on the wall. If it is cool to the touch, it is most likely made of plaster; drywall will be closer to room temperature. Drywall will have a hollow sound if you knock on it, and a plaster wall will sound more solid.

LOCATING WALL STUDS

To support the shelf, you will need to either find a stud in the wall or use the proper wall anchors to support the screws. This is easily accomplished with an inexpensive, battery-operated stud finder, available at most hardware and home supply stores. Here are the steps:

1. Using a level, lightly mark the underside of where the shelf will go with a pencil.
2. Drag your stud finder over the pencil line and it should beep at the edge of the stud. If you have a plaster wall, you will need to set your stud finder to the "deep scan" mode. Most studs are 16 inches apart unless you live in an older home, in which case the studs can be anywhere from 18 to 20 inches apart.
3. Use a pencil to mark the center of the stud. You will likely need to adjust the shelf slightly to the left or right to have the brackets look even. In most cases, you may catch one or two studs along the line depending on the length of your shelf, and the other brackets will have to be secured using a wall anchor.
4. Use a pencil to mark the holes of the brackets. This is where you will place your screws or anchors.

Place your bracket in the middle of the stud and up to the shelf line. Place wood screws directly through the holes of the bracket catching the studs. Use 1½–2-inch wood screws.

ANCHORS

If your bracket marks don't line up to a stud, you will need to use an anchor. If you have drywall, screw-in anchors are the easiest and fastest anchors to use. They fit right on the end of your No. 2 Phillips head screwdriver and screw directly into the drywall. Screw-in anchors come in various sizes, and they make it easy to redecorate because you can easily remove them and patch up the holes.

For those of you who have plaster walls, you will need to use a toggle anchor if you don't catch a stud. Toggle anchors are the machine screws with the "propeller-looking" metal piece that collapses when pinched together. Using a drill bit, drill at the pencil marks you made for the holes of the bracket. Put the toggle screws through the holes of the bracket and twirl the little toggle onto the screw with the collapsible end facing toward the head of the screw. Once it pushes all the way in, the toggle releases and springs open. Your screw needs to be long enough to penetrate the thickness of the wall (which is about 1 inch for a plaster wall) and have room for the length of the toggle wing. A 2¼-inch toggle screw will usually do the job.

With your bracket up against the wall and the toggles pushed into the holes, you will need to work one screw at a time. Pull the screw toward you as you turn your screwdriver. You need to have the wings of the toggle firmly against the back of the wall so that it doesn't spin on you when you're screwing it in. This may feel a bit awkward since you will be pulling the screw toward you as you are turning the screw with a screwdriver. Tighten up both screws.

If the shelf is between two walls, then you can use cleats—wooden supports made of 1 × 4, 1 × 3, or 1 × 2 lumber. They hold up a shelf by supporting the ends and the back of the shelf. Again, use your level to draw a straight line where you want the shelf to go. Attach the cleats to your walls with a wood screw (2½ inches), catching the studs where you can find them, and use screw-in anchors for drywall or toggle anchors for plaster walls where you can't find studs. When you have a shelf between two walls but longer than about 2 feet, you can use one or two brackets underneath it along the back wall to help support the weight.

Once you get the hang of hanging shelves, you will want to install them everywhere—especially when you realize how easy it is to do, how organized you will feel, and how much money you've saved because you did it yourself!

43

FOLD FITTED SHEETS

ERIK DEMAINE

*Dr. Erik Demaine is an associate professor in Electrical
Engineering and Computer Science at the Massachusetts
Institute of Technology. At age twenty he became the youngest
professor ever to teach at MIT. He is a pioneer in the field of
computational origami, the study of complex geometrical
problems through the art of paper folding.*

$\mathbf{F}$itted sheets are those sheets with elastic bands embedded in
their periphery, making for stretchy, poofy corners. These sheets
are great for locking on to your bed, never to come off until you
need to wash them (or until a really rough night). But what they
never seem to do is fold right. They bunch up in strange ways that
cause them to be several times thicker and sloppier than a normally folded sheet (repeatedly folded in half and/or thirds in both
directions). I have a friend whose family won't even buy fitted
sheets because they can't stand unruly linens littering the closet.

Fear not—there is an origamic trick to folding fitted sheets
that prevents the disorderly bunching and restores order to your
closet.

1. Start with the sheet on a flat surface (e.g., a bed), with the ruffling of the corners sticking up.

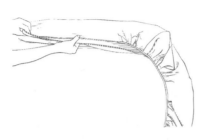

2. Fold the sheet in half lengthwise, reducing the long side in half.

3. Turn the ruffling of each of the two corners you just folded inside out.

4. Tuck each of those inside-out corners into the inside-in corner underneath.

5. Fold the three unfolded sides of the sheet (those next to the corners) in a little, to roughly match the length of the stitched seam in the corners. The amount to fold the sides varies significantly from sheet to sheet. Get to know your sheets by trying different amounts to get the next two steps to work.

6. Pinch the two pairs of corners to make two little triangles sticking up out of the flat surface.

7. Fold the two triangles toward the top of the sheet so they are flat against the same side of the sheet. If done properly, an edge of each triangle should meet the side of the sheet, and the entire folded

sheet should become a nice, flat rectangle. This step is the hardest, but with practice you'll see how to adjust the folded edges to make this step work out for your fitted sheets.

8. Fold the sheet in half crosswise, reducing the short side in half, and bringing together the two pairs of corners.
9. Fold the sheet in thirds lengthwise, first folding the thicker part to the center, and then folding the opposite end on top of the thick part.

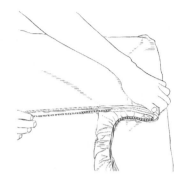

The last two steps can be varied to fold in half/thirds/repeatedly crosswise and lengthwise, just like regular sheet folding, to suit your sheet size and desired folded size. But I find this combination best for making a clean final rectangle (at least for double and queen beds).

The expert folder will probably want to perform the first four steps in the air—folding the sheet in half and tucking two corners into the other two corners—before laying the sheet on a flat surface. This method has the advantage of requiring half as much flat space for folding.

If you're having trouble with the tricky step 7, or are just curious about how it works, you might try the origami version of the same phenomenon. Take a piece of paper, cut out a small square from the corner with two cuts, and tape together the two cut edges. The result is a corner of a square paper tray, which roughly represents the ruffled corner of fitted sheets. Now fold the two edges of the tray and pinch the corner, and you'll get a proper right triangle sticking up. Flatten the triangle down against one of the edges, and it will meet that edge exactly. Mimic this origami principle in your sheet foldings, and you'll have a beautifully neat closet that will shock my friend's family.

44

CONTROL CLUTTER

PETER WALSH

Peter Walsh is the professional organizer on the TLC

hit show Clean Sweep *and the author of* How to

Organize Just About Everything.

I f the very thought of getting organized makes your palms sweat and your stomach queasy, you are not alone! Most clutter is accumulated over years, so the prospect of de-cluttering can be overwhelming even to the strong of heart.

Keep in mind that a richer life comes from living in a space that supports and sustains us. Clutter sucks the life, the spirit, and the creativity out of any space. Getting organized is a sure first step to a better life. Here are a few simple steps to get you started:

1. *Before you rush into organizing, spend some time thinking about the type of life you want to live.* Make a list of your priorities and your goals. Then look around at your material possessions in your living space and your work space. Ask yourself whether these items add or detract from what it is you want from life. Remember—more is not necessarily better!

2. *Decide what stays and what goes.* Make a commitment to keep only those things that contribute to a richer life. Honor and respect those things that you value as important.

3. *Start slow—but just start!* It's taken months—or maybe even years—for your space to become cluttered, so it's unrealistic to try and organize everything in one day or even a weekend. Instead, start small—one room or section of a room at a time. Make a commitment every day to de-clutter another part of your home.

4. *Apply specific strategies depending on the area you are tackling or the items involved.* Within a very short period you will see definite progress.

   * For clothes, books, or shoes try the ratio rule. For every four items you keep, discard one. Challenge yourself and try to lower the ratio to 3 to 1 or, if you are really brave, 2 to 1.

   * For general clutter try the two-a-day technique. Every day for a week (or a month!) fill one garbage bag with trash and one with items that you intend to donate to charity or pass onto someone else.

   * Just to prove that you wear 20 percent of your clothes 80 percent of the time, try the clothes hanger trick. Reverse the way your clothes are hung in your closet. When you wear and return an item, replace the hanger the correct way around. At the end of 3 or 6 months, you can clearly see from the hangers still hung in reverse what you haven't worn and, most likely, what you can live without.

   * For bills, receipts, and paperwork you need to keep, use an inexpensive 12-month accordion file. This will help to quickly and easily organize your monthly receipts and paid bills. At the end of 12 months discard the oldest bills and receipts.

5. *Think of your space in terms of zones.* Have a specific area for bills and paperwork, for your clothes, for cleaning items, for the books and magazines that you read, even for your car keys. By keeping like things together in a specific area, you'll find it easier to locate the items you need and to stay organized.

6. *If it all gets to be too much, find a de-cluttering buddy.* An honest friend will help you put things in perspective and help you part with that neon jumpsuit from 1982.

7. *Understand that it's not always about the stuff.* Don't be too hard on yourself. Recognize that clutter is often a reflection of something deeper that might be troubling you. Dealing with the clutter will open up not only the physical space in your life but also your emotional, psychological, and spiritual space as well.

45

DO A SPRING CLEANING

TARA ARONSON

Tara Aronson, aka Mrs. Clean Jeans, is the author of two books, including Mrs. Clean Jeans' Housekeeping with Kids. *She is an "everyday emergency expert" on Fine Living's* Simplify Your Life *program, and her column,* Coming Clean, *appears twice monthly in the* San Francisco Chronicle.

As a modern mom with three busy kids and two perfect cats (except for the fact that they shed year-round), I'm all for a clean house with a healthy environment for my family to eat, sleep, chase catnip, and chase one another in. But I have an aversion to the whole-house, blast-everything-with-heavy-cleaning-products spring cleaning. So I've compiled this guide of less-toxic methods.

REDUCING YOUR BELONGINGS

The prime reason most of us avoid spring cleaning is that we've got too much stuff. Before you can clean anything, you'll need to reduce your belongings. Toss what you don't use, don't need, or don't want. Have your kids do the same. Don't plan on purging the house in a Saturday morning. Allot at least a half day per room.

FURNITURE STAIN REMOVAL GUIDE

Big-ticket items like furniture and upholstery should be cleaned seasonally—at least. It's the only way to control the airborne cooking oils and dust that inevitably settle on these pieces. Whether it is your daughter's chocolate snack sweetening the ottoman or Grandma's makeup smudges on the sofa, busting these and other stains is a piece of cake.

GREASE

To remove gravy, butter, dressing, olive oil, vegetable oils, and other mystery spills, blot on a small amount of rubbing alcohol. Repeat until there is no more transfer of stain to white cloth or plain white paper towel. If the stain is gone, stop here. If not, blot with a solution of 1 teaspoon dishwashing liquid or laundry detergent and 1 cup warm water. Work from outside of stain toward the center. Rinse with a damp sponge to remove detergent. Blot dry and rinse with solution of ½ cup vinegar and ½ cup water. Blot dry. Brush when fully dry to restore texture.

PROTEINS

To remove dairy product, egg, grass, blood, and urine stains, blot with a solution of 1 teaspoon dishwashing liquid and 1 cup warm water. Repeat. Rinse with vinegar solution of 1 cup white vinegar and 1 cup warm water. Blot dry. Brush fabric when fully dry. Blot milk spills with a small amount of dry-cleaning fluid and blot dry. Repeat until no stain transfers to paper towel.

TANNINS

To remove fruit juice, wine, soft-drink, coffee, ketchup, and tomato-sauce stains, wet fabric slightly and let set, damp, about one minute. Blot with paper towel. Repeat until no stain is evident on towel and blot dry. If stain is gone, stop here. If not, rub in a detergent solution of 1 teaspoon dishwashing liquid and 1 cup warm water. Repeat until no stain transfers to towel.

Tip: always pretest cleaning solution on an inconspicuous area of the upholstery or furniture.

PETS

They're our best friends, but you don't have to live with their pungent reminders. Their stains and strong smells can be removed, especially if you catch them when they're still fresh.

LITTER BOX ODOR

Use clay-based clumping kitty litter to absorb odors. If that doesn't knock out odors, clean out the cat box with ½ cup vinegar.

PET URINE ON CARPET AND UPHOLSTERY

First, soak up as much as you can with a white rag or paper towels. Blot on a solution of ¼ teaspoon mild liquid laundry detergent and 1 cup warm water. Repeat until there is no more of the stain transferring to a towel or rag. If that doesn't work, try blotting with a solution of 2 teaspoons ammonia and 1 cup water. Rinse with warm water. Repeat. Blot dry. If that doesn't work, try blotting the area with a solution of 1 cup white vinegar and 2 cups water. Cover with several layers of paper towels weighted down with a heavy, nonfading object. Continue changing paper towels until the carpet is dry. If you can't remove the stain, consider re-covering the furniture.

FECES ON CARPET AND UPHOLSTERY

Gently scoop away excess with a spoon or spatula. Blot with the same ammonia solution that is used on pet urine (see above). Let it soak for several minutes. Blot and repeat until the stain is removed. Rinse with cold water. Blot dry.

PET HAIR ON CARPET AND SOFA

On the carpet, use a vacuum with a good beater brush or brush roll. Regular vacuums don't generate enough suction to pick up all the pet hair from the carpet. Or run a squeegee over the area. Just swipe it over the carpet and watch it cling to the brush. On upholstered sofas and chairs, use a pet rake, a special brush with crimped nylon bristles. Use light, even strokes to remove the fur. Velour brushes, tape rollers, and even tape wrapped around your hand also work. Both pet supply and home stores sell "pet sponges," which are used dry on carpets and upholstered furniture.

Tip: avoid using steam cleaners to clean urine odors from carpet or upholstery. The heat will permanently set the odor and the stain by bonding the protein into any man-made fibers.

46

HAVE A TAG SALE

KRISTIN VAN OGTROP

Kristin van Ogtrop is managing editor of Real Simple
magazine. Real Simple *created Get Organized
New York, the city's largest tag sale ever.*

Having a tag sale is a great way to de-clutter your living space and make a bit of cash. Some believe it's also a great way to meet people, but I have yet to meet anyone at a tag sale whom I'd like to know longer than a day or two. After all, tag sales are a competitive sport.

When you are throwing a tag sale, therefore, you need to have a tough constitution. Think NFL referee. The attendees will be poring over your possessions, things you may actually have once loved, and scrutinizing everything with a cold, dispassionate eye. You need to check your own emotions at the door.

If you're confident that you have the fortitude to hold a tag sale, there are a few issues you should consider before you begin:

WHAT TO SELL

If you haven't used it or worn it in two years, sell it. If you hate it but are keeping it because it was a gift, sell it. (Just make sure the giver does not attend the sale.) If it doesn't fit or doesn't match or doesn't work, sell it. (But if it doesn't work, make sure that is indicated on the price tag. "Buyer beware" may be the unofficial tag sale motto, but you don't want to be a jerk.)

GETTING THE WORD OUT

Place an item in the Classifieds section of your local paper on the Thursday or Friday before a weekend sale. Do you want "early birds"? If not, specify that clearly in your ad. If you do—and you don't mind people loitering in your front yard an hour or two before the official start of the sale—consider charging a small fee (such as $10) to allow early birds first dibs.

WEATHER CONCERNS

If there is a chance of rain (and there almost always is), set a rain date in advance. Make sure you have a permanent marker on hand to make big, weather-resistant signs to lure customers on the sale day. The bigger and brighter, the better. Remember, arrows are a universally understood symbol.

Once the day arrives—with any luck, a sunny and windless day with temperatures in the mid-70s—remember to do the following:

* Have a lock box on hand with $100 worth of change, including lots of singles and coins.
* Decide in advance how you feel about negotiating, and stick to that decision—at least until you see what isn't selling.
* Have a pile designated "Free" to draw more people to your sale. However, use this word with great discretion.
* Tag everything else with a clear price; many people will walk away before asking a price.

* Consider lowering the price (or at least relaxing any no-negotiating rule) if an item doesn't sell after a few hours.
* Group like items together to help sale navigation (as well as the quirky collector who is dying to buy, say, the eight Boz Scaggs albums you have been holding on to since 1983).

After your sale is over, you are guaranteed to feel both shock at what people bought and disappointment at what they didn't. This, of course, brings us back to that tough constitution. You can handle the surprise, and you can handle the rejection. And armed with your experience, you can certainly handle having another sale next year.

47

STOCK A TOOLBOX

NORMA VALLY

Norma Vally is host of Toolbelt Diva *on Discovery Home
Channel and* Toolbelt Diva *on Discovery Channel Radio.
She is the author of* Chix Can Fix.

I approach buying tools with passion and savvy—much the way I shoe shop. My mantra guiding me through the tool corral is *you get what you pay for.* Your initial thought may be, "Hey, I only need this tool (shoe) for one project (party), so why spend a lot?" The truth is projects always come up (as do social functions) and a high-quality tool (shoe) will go the distance (dance floor). Cheap tools don't perform well—plastic cracks, heads strip (heels break off!)—and what should be a functional fix turns into a frustrating fiasco (blisters).

You may not need to buy the most expensive tool on the shelf, but research brands, look for tools with warranties, and look at what pros load in their toolbelts.

Quality in mind, start stocking with these five must-have tools:

1. *16-ounce hammer:* This is the perfect all-purpose hammer. It's light enough so it won't strain your wrist, yet heavy enough so you're not undergunned.

2. *25-foot-long 1-inch-wide tape measure:* I love this tape measure because it's fat, an inch wide. This width allows you to easily read the numbers, and it won't bend when you pull it out past a few feet.

3. *Tongue and groove pliers:* These pliers are adjustable, easy to control, and will fit around various size fittings and nuts.

4. *Retractable utility knife (with blade storage in handle):* You'll use this knife to cut everything from carpet to drywall. It's also easy to replace the blade, and the blade storage handle is superconvenient.

5. *Ratcheting screwdriver with multiple bits:* The multiple bits change out easily whether you need a Phillips, slotted, or square drive. The ratcheting action allows you to keep steady pressure while simply twisting the handle in place.

As you become more proficient with these tools, your confidence level will build, enabling you to take on more complicated projects. In your excitement, don't go crazy trying to buy every available tool. Instead, buy tools that are project specific. For example, if you're ready to tackle a more intense electric project, get yourself lineman's pliers and wire strippers. Your tool collection should grow gradually along with your skill level.

There's nothing like a trip to the emergency room to knock the fun right out of fixing! The following are your five must-have safety tools/accessories:

1. *Safety goggles:* These glasses should fit properly so they don't slide off your face when you lean over. They should comply with OSHA regulations.

2. *Mask:* Mask type should be project specific. For a light project, a dust mask will suffice. Using a harsh chemical, for instance, may warrant a respirator. Always check safety recommendations on your product label.

3. *Work gloves:* Glove type should be task related. For example, a waterproof glove should be worn if using a wet, caustic product (always check safety recommendations). Also, a snug fit is crucial, especially if you're using a power tool with a spinning blade—loose gloves are notorious for getting caught in moving parts.
4. *Ear protection:* Any time you're working and you have to yell over the noise from your project in order to be heard, you need ear protection. Be it plugs or muffs, ear safety is a must to prevent hearing loss.
5. *Electricity testers:* Flipping a breaker isn't enough—a neon tester or plug-in circuit analyzer will ensure that there is no electricity flowing so you can work safely.

It's always good to have these *miscellaneous items* stocked in your box:

* lubricating spray
* assorted nails, screws, and anchors
* masking, duct, and electrical tape
* sandpaper
* zip-ties
* flashlight
* long-reach lighter
* permanent marker and carpenter pencil

Truth be told, as much as I love to open my closet doors and see a brand-new designer shoebox, it's the well-stocked toolbox in my closet that gets me on my feet and ready to tackle projects skillfully and safely for decades. Not even Prada can do that.

48

SILENCE A SQUEAKY FLOOR

Tom Kraeutler

Tom Kraeutler is the host of The Money Pit, *a nationally syndicated home improvement radio show. He was named one of the "100 Most Important Talk Show Hosts in America" by* Talkers Magazine. *He is a frequent contributor to CNN and is the remodeling columnist for* House Beautiful *magazine.*

While a floor squeak is annoying, it seldom means you have an underlying structural problem. Floor squeaks occur when loose floors move as you walk over them and they can happen in homes that are brand-new or very old. The actual sound stems from one or a combination of two sources: either loose floorboards are rubbing together or the nails that hold down the floor are squeaking as they move in and out of their holes.

Fortunately, squeaks can be about as easy to fix as they are to find—if you know what to do. The solution to both scenarios is to resecure the floor to the floor joists (the beams that floors are nailed to). Here's what to do:

CARPETED FLOORS

When it comes to fixing squeaks under a carpet, the best solution is always to remove the carpet. Once it's removed, use hardened drywall screws to hold the floor in place by driving one next to every nail in the floor. Screws never pull out so they are more reliable than nails.

If removing wall-to-wall carpet is too much for you to tackle, there's a method that may allow you to fix the squeak from above. Using a stud finder, locate the floor joist beneath the carpet in the area of the squeak. Usually, joists run perpendicular to the front and back walls of a home so check in that direction first. Once you've located the joist, drive a 10d or 12d galvanized finish nail through the carpet, through the subfloor and into the floor joist. You'll probably need to do this in two or three places. Make sure to drive the nail in at a slight angle as this will help prevent the floor from getting loose again. Last, grab the carpet by the nap or pile and pull it up until the head of the finish nail passes through it. As the nails disappear through the carpet, so should the squeaks.

HARDWOOD FLOORS

Fixing squeaking hardwood floors is a little trickier than fixing a carpeted floor, but the principles remain the same. Locate the area of the squeak and then use a stud finder to locate the joists. Note that since the joists will be 1–1½ inches under the hardwood floor, you'll need to use a stud finder that has a "deep scan" feature to be sure you are in the right spot. Once you've identified the location, you can either screw down the loose area or renail it as suggested above with the carpet.

In either case, you'll need to predrill the floor. For screws, purchase a bit from your local home center or hardware store that includes a counter bore. This will leave a hole that is exactly three-eighths of an inch in diameter and the perfect size to fill with an easily available oak plug. If you are nailing the floor, use a drill bit that is slightly smaller in diameter than the finish nails you are using. This way, the nails will pass easily through the floor without bending or splitting floorboards.

Squeaking floors may be one of life's little annoyances, but they are easily kept under control. And if squeaks ever really get under your skin, remember the technical term for them: charm!

49

REFINISH A BASEMENT

KITTY BARTHOLOMEW

Kitty Bartholomew is frequently called television's first reality

decorator. She is the former decorating expert of ABC TV's

The Home Show *and HGTV's* Kitty Bartholomew:

You're Home. *She is the author of* Kitty Bartholomew's

Decorating Style: A Hands-On Approach to Creating

Affordable, Beautiful, and Comfortable Rooms.

Nearly all basements begin their lives with two drawbacks: the surfaces are hard and cold, and the environment is dark and dank. Our mission is to counteract those tendencies, which can render a basement too clammy and uncomfortable to inhabit for any length of time.

Here are some ideas for making a basement a place you want to be:

WALL TREATMENTS

I favor a natural-looking material on the walls, to temper the hardness of concrete or cinder block. I recommend staying away from wallpaper, as basement walls tend to wick moisture from the surrounding earth, and wallpaper will curl up. If you paint the walls, look for a mildew-resistant paint or primer. For colors, I suggest staying away from cool colors such as blues and greens and going for warmer shades such as terra-cotta, salmon, or my own personal favorite color, red. White is way too cold and hard a color. Even though you want to lighten up the space, white is not the answer.

LIGHTING

Basements are by nature dark. If there are windows, they are high and narrow, so artificial lighting will be critical for creating a welcoming environment. Stay away from fluorescent, which can give off a bluish tint and cause the room to feel cold. Instead, use halogen lights, which are closest to the tones of natural lights, or incandescent. Can lights built into a dropped ceiling can flood the area with light and can be supplemented with floor and table lamps with amber-colored shades that cast a warm glow. The dropped ceiling can also hide the pipes and plumbing that give many basements a clammy, yucky feeling.

MIRRORS

Most people tend to use mirrors to make spaces look bigger or wider. But what they do best is reflect natural light back into a room. That means you want to place mirrors opposite a natural light source. This is especially critical in a basement, where natural light is minimal. Wherever there is a window, hang a large mirror on the opposite wall. Then you're effectively doubling the natural light, almost like adding another window.

FLOORING

The trick underfoot is to soften the experience without the risk of adding expensive carpeting that could get damaged by flooding. After all, if there is ever a plumbing overflow in your house—think water-heater malfunction, washing machine disaster, or run-of-the mill toilet trouble—the water will follow a downward course right into the basement. You want to be able to take up the carpet and allow it to dry. Rather than tacked-down carpeting, go for area rugs, even layered to add interest. Many Oriental rugs these days are made from olefin and polypropylene, two materials that defy mildew. And think about polishing or waxing your concrete floor to give it a warm patina. Concrete floors have never been so chic, and your basement floor may be waiting for its own makeover.

STORAGE

Here's a really clever idea for using the space below the basement stairs. You get a bookcase that is as wide as the stairs, and that will fit under one of the higher stair risers. You install four casters on the bottom of the bookcase and then you slide it sideways into the space under the stairs, with the side of the bookcase facing out. You install a handle, like you'd find on a cabinet door, to slide the bookcase in and out as needed. Store your DVDs here, or books or games. How clever is that?

FURNITURE

Your older upholstered pieces might end up in the basement as you purchase new pieces for the living room or den. But if you can buy furniture specifically for the basement, go for pieces that are not fully upholstered. Think rattan or bamboo or wicker with cushions. Then, when the cushions become musty after a long, cold winter, you can let them air outside on the first sunny day of spring.

50

INSTALL A DOGGIE DOOR

RON HAZELTON

Ron Hazelton is the host of Ron Hazelton's HouseCalls *and the*
Home Improvement Editor for Good Morning America. *He is*
the author of Ron Hazelton's HouseCalls: America's Most
Requested Home Improvement Projects.

We're calling it a doggie door, but a pet portal works equally
well for Miss Kitty, Peter Rabbit, or Porky the Potbelly Pig. For
simplicity's sake, though, let's assume it is a canine companion
who's getting unrestricted, 24/7 access to your home.

Although I have not taken a survey, I imagine most folks
choose to place their pooch's entry smack in the middle of an
existing human doorway. Now, there's nothing wrong with this,
but you do end up with a hole in your door that's not particularly
attractive and may not impress a prospective buyer who happens
to be petless. So, here are a couple of alternatives.

If you have a glass sliding door, a pet *panel* might be the way
to go. They're easy to install, require no structural modifications,
and can be taken with you when you move.

Another option is a through-the-wall door. I know what
you're thinking: "Are you crazy, make a hole in the side of my

house?" But these go in fairly easily. You cut openings in the outside and inside walls, install an outer and inner frame, and connect the two with a sort of "tunnel" that comes with the door kit. If the floor inside your home is substantially higher than the ground outside, you'll need to install a ramp to give your pet access to his private entrance.

Should you want to conceal the exterior opening from view, set a doghouse in front of it. Naturally, you'll have to add a rear entrance to the pooch palace, so Fido can leave your house, enter his, and then exit through his own front door.

So you've considered the options and decided to go with the door-in-door approach. Here are a few tips. For starters, I recommend taking the door off its hinges and laying it on a couple of sawhorses. Trust me, putting the door in a horizontal position makes this job easier and one you can do with two hands instead of three or four.

Outline the area where the doggie device will go with masking tape, then make your layout marks on the tape. The lines will be more visible and you'll avoid having to remove extraneous pencil lead from your entry door.

Deciding where to place the pet door really depends on doggie's dimensions. Here are a couple of rules of thumb: the bottom of the door opening should equal the distance from the ground to your dog's underbelly, and the center of the door opening ought to be level with your dog's shoulders. Pet doors come in a variety of sizes from small (Pekingese) to extra large (Doberman), so be sure to match portal to pooch.

The easiest and neatest way to cut the opening is to drill half-inch holes at the corners, insert the blade of a jig saw, and go from one hole to the next.

Once your pup's passageway is installed, you'll need to train him to use it. Wait until he wants to go outside, and then pull the flap open and tease him through with a favorite treat. Each time your dog walks through, lay the flap gently on his back so he gets used to the feeling.

Finally, to keep stray cats, raccoons, and other animals from sharing your pet's passageway, you may want a security door. Some use a latch that's activated by a magnet worn on your dog's collar. Others have a small motor that opens the door when your pet approaches wearing a tiny transmitter.

51

KEEP YOUR PET CLEAN

CHARLOTTE REED

Charlotte Reed is a columnist for Dog Fancy *and* Pet Business *magazines. She authored the* Pet-Owning Made Easy *series of booklets. She owns Two Dogs & A Goat Incorporated, a comprehensive Manhattan-based pet-care service.*

Although we love our pets, we need to spend a lot of time cleaning up after them because they can't clean up after themselves. By keeping our pets clean, we keep our homes clean.

BRUSHING

To avoid unwanted pet hair on you and household surfaces, brush your pet regularly. Brushing removes loose hair, dead skin, dirt, and odor from your pet's fur and helps to distribute natural oils throughout your pet's coat. For cats, habitual brushing keeps their digestive tract healthy by preventing hair balls.

Frequency of brushing your dog or cat depends upon its coat. For pets with shorter hair, brush them weekly. For those with longer hair, coiffing sessions must be more frequent or even daily. If your animal does not like to be brushed, try using a grooming glove or a rubber curry brush. If possible, brush your pet outside in order to prevent dander particles that contribute to allergies from being airborne. If you hire a dog walker or pet sitter, make brushing part of the pet professional's regular routine.

BATHING

Timing of a bath should depend upon the arrival of that unique pet smell that can cause unpleasant or embarrassing odors in your home or that very dirty incident that requires that your pet be washed immediately. In the long run, it is much easier to start bathing your pet when it is in infancy to allow it to acclimate to a regular grooming regimen. Bathe a dog once a month and a cat a few times a year.

Before bathing, always brush and comb your dog or cat thoroughly. To prepare, have the following supplies ready: pet shampoo and conditioner, hose attachment, and one or two towels. You may also wish to use a rubber mat to prevent slipping and a leash and collar so that your pet is less likely to jump out of the tub or sink before you are done.

To begin, use cotton balls to plug the ears. Next, wet and shampoo the body and the legs. Don't rub; instead, massage shampoo into a lather to avoid pet's hair from tangling. Shampoo your pet's head last, taking care not to get the shampoo into its eyes, ears, and nose. Leave shampoo on for 2 to 3 minutes, while speaking calmly and massaging your pet for its comfort. Rinse thoroughly 3 or 4 times to remove all the shampoo. Conditioning your pet's coat is optional but encouraged. When you are done bathing, towel dry your animal by blotting the coat. Comb and brush once again to make sure there are no tangles. If you prefer, finish with a nice blow-dry on a warm setting.

If you cannot bathe your pet, visit the groomer on a regular basis and use pet wipes to keep him fresh in between baths.

POSSESSIONS

Clean pet beds, toys, and clothing will contribute to a healthier pet and a clean and tidy home. Purchase beds, toys, and clothing that are easy to wash and dry. Machine-wash and thoroughly dry all pet beds. Although some toys can be put in the dishwasher, others should be put in a lingerie or garment bag for machine washing. Dry toys thoroughly and make sure no water remains inside them. Machine-wash coats and sweaters but hang dry to avoid shrinkage. Like you, your pet likes to sleep in a fresh bed, and have spotless clothing and dirt-free possessions.

FEEDING

Feeding your pet out of a clean ceramic or stainless steel dish is a matter of hygiene and easier clean-up. Wash pet bowls in a dishwasher or by hand in the sink and rinse thoroughly before drying with a paper towel. To avoid unnecessary spills from kicked food bowls, feed pets in a utility room or in an out-of-the-way area with an easy-to-clean surface. After your pet's last meal, wipe the surface with a gentle pet-friendly cleaner.

52

CLEAN GUTTERS

MICHAEL HOLIGAN

Michael Holigan is the host of the nationally syndicated Michael
Holigan's Your New House *television show on the Discovery
Channel. He is the president of Holigan Family Holdings Ltd.,
a Dallas-based company offering tips and advice on how to
build, buy, and remodel houses.*

There is nothing quite as beautiful as a tree, and nothing that
leaves as big a mess to clean up (except maybe kids). The real
problem occurs when those leaves start clogging up your gutters.
Your gutters are only about 3 inches deep, so it doesn't take many
leaves to cause a dam that any beaver would be proud of. And once
the rainwater starts backing up in your gutters, the water is going
to start flowing over the sides until the weight finally pulls the gutters off your house. The rain is then going to come straight off
your roof in sheets and destroy any plants and landscaping below
until you pay someone a big fee to install new gutters.

There are easy ways and hard ways to keep the gutters clean.
We will start easy. You need a ladder and a whisk broom on a
dry day. If the leaves are dry, you can easily sweep them out and
over the edge. Notice "over the edge." I know it seems silly to

have to spell it out, but don't sweep them onto your roof, as they will be back in your gutter in a few hours. You will be amazed at what I have seen homeowners do.

The second option is a leaf blower. If the leaves are dry and you have a low pitch on your roof, you can walk along the edge with a leaf blower and blast them out of there. This is the fastest way but probably also the most dangerous if you are not careful. If you don't want to get on the roof, use the leaf blower while on a ladder.

The broom and the leaf blower are not going to work if the leaves are wet. If this is the case, you will need a spatula that fits inside the gutter—not a big one but one that is the same width as the bottom of the gutter. You need to get all of the leaves out, not just the ones on the top.

Once you get the gutters cleaned out, you may find out that the water still backs up. That means you have a clog in your downspouts. This is normally caused by broken sticks and branches that get lodged in there and then leaves that catch on them. In my home, clogs in downspouts are caused by model airplanes and other kids' toys that can be shot, thrown, or lobbed up onto the roof. Invariably, they will wash into the gutter and get lodged into the downspout.

The easiest way to break up these clogs is a plumber snake (an auger), a long piece of steel on a reel that plumbers use in toilets and sewer lines to break up clogs. You can pick one up at any hardware store. Take it to the top of the downspout and start uncoiling the snake. If you can't break all the way through the clog, shift to the bottom of the downspout and work the other direction. If you keep working it back and forth from top to bottom, you will, eventually, break through any clog.

Now, before you put up the ladder, place the hose in the highest part of the gutter and turn on the water. The water should be coming out of the bottom of the downspout as fast as it is coming out of the hose. When the leaves start to fall, do a visual check every week to make sure that it is clear up there. The rest of the year should be fine.

53

TRIM HEDGES

ROGER COOK

Roger Cook is the landscape contractor for the This Old House

and Ask This Old House *television series and serves on the*

editorial board of This Old House *magazine. He is the owner of*

K & R Tree and Landscape Company, based in Massachusetts.

Pruning shrubs is a science that anyone can master after learning a few simple steps. I recommend starting with a plant in the back of the bunch or a fast-growing plant. This gives you a victim to sacrifice as you hone your technique. It is important to spend time learning the growth habit of the plant you are pruning and not to rush!

The first scientific thing we need to understand is apical dominance, the process through which the bud on the end of a branch releases a hormone that limits interior buds from developing. When this happens, a plant will grow in a natural shape. Pruning eliminates apical dominance, allowing dormant buds to become active and grow, causing the plant to get so thick that it keeps sunlight from getting into the shrub and prevents interior growth. Proper pruning involves a balance between enabling some sunlight to get in and curbing shrubs at the same time.

TOOLS

Hand pruners will cut most branches up to ½ inch thick, depending on the strength of your hands. There are two types: *bypass* pruners and *anvil* pruners. I think of bypass pruners as my fine cutlery and use them only for my fine pruning. I use anvil pruners for pruning out dead wood and branches that are down in the ground or mulch. Once a branch gets over ½ inch thick, I switch to *loppers*. These come with either bypass or anvil blades. For shrub pruning, loppers with shorter handles work better in small places. When cutting low branches, use long-handled loppers.

Shears are long-handled cutters with two long blades that bypass each other, giving you a large cutting area. They are useful for formal hedges and are also responsible for bizarre shapes like globes, squares, and triangles, as well as shrubs that need to be pruned exactly like last year's shearing. When you buzz cut a shrub with shears, all of the dormant buds are stimulated (apical dominance!), so there is no interior growth to cut back to, and the shrub increases in size each year.

Now let's look at where to make cuts. When possible, you want

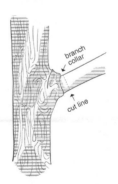

to prune at the main stem or where branches meet. Cuts at the main trunk should leave the branch collar (the raised area attaching a branch to the tree) intact. This branch collar helps shrubs heal quickly. Flush cuts, on the other hand, remove the collar and take longer to heal. When pruning a hedge, always attach a string line to two stakes, giving you a height at which to cut evenly. Keep the top narrower than the bottom to allow sunlight to get to the bottom branches.

FLOWERING SHRUBS

The golden rule of pruning flowering shrubs is to do it the day after the flowers turn brown, not before the plant has flowered! By pruning then, the shrub will still have time to set flower buds by the following year.

EVERGREENS

The ideal time to prune evergreens is in early spring before they start growing. This way you can prune openings into them that will allow light to get in and develop new growth. This will keep the plant a nice shape and size. Most evergreens end up getting sheared in the summer when we have time to do it, but this will keep them off-color the rest of the year!

CUT BACK SHRUBS

Certain shrubs flower on new growth. Examples include hibiscus, spirea, and potentilla. These shrubs are easy to maintain and can be cut back down to a foot tall or, in some cases, to the ground level and will sprout out and flower that year.

RENOVATION PRUNING

When a plant has outgrown its place, it is time for renovation pruning. To take any large shrub and reduce its size, use the three-year rule. The first year, remove a third of the oldest stems. This allows for sunlight to come in and promote new growth while the plant still looks good. The second year, remove the second third of the old stems and the third year remove the final third. You will be left with a shrub that looks great, is full of new growth, and is reduced in size.

CLEAN UP

You can lay down a tarp or use a barrel to catch clippings as they fall. Be sure to put the clippings in a compost pile rather than in the trash.

When you are done with your pruning, clean off your tools, sharpen them, and spray with a rust inhibitor.

Pruning is necessary to keep plants healthy, in check, or from outgrowing their space, and even if it is done badly, like a bad haircut, sooner or later it will grow back.

TO BEAUTIFY

54

KEEP A HOME
SMELLING FRESH

Jo Malone

Jo Malone is the founder of Jo Malone, a line of personal-care

products with an emphasis on fragrance. Jo Malone stores are

located in central London and across the United States. Malone

is known for her innovative concepts and philosophies, and she is

the first perfumer to introduce living colognes, a single scent

that can be used on the skin or to scent fabrics and the air.

Bringing scent into the home is not just the finishing touch to creating a certain ambience or evoking a mood to suit particular rooms; it's also a subconscious way to appeal to the senses. It's a creative process that can be as simple as a well-placed vase of sweet-smelling flowers or a more complex combination of scents that change as you move through your home.

Here are my top five tips to invite scent into your home:

1. FLOWERS: For a sophisticated look and easy way to scent the home, buy a bunch of flowers that are all the same type, choosing white blooms that have a powerful and long-lasting scent

(such as lily, long-stemmed roses, or amaryllis). Place the flowers in a clear glass vase in a central spot so the scent can radiate through the room. Alternatively, use a dramatic single-stem flower such as a tuberose that, on its own, will scent a large area. One huge vase of eucalyptus looks great on the dining room table, is a stunning centerpiece, and makes the house smell amazing.

2. SCENTED CANDLES: Combine scented candles of various fragrances to create ambience. For an oasis of calm, orange blossom mixed with the scent of figs or lime is perfect. For dinner parties, use an eclectic mix of scents throughout the evening: amber and coffee scents are welcoming, grapefruit clears away food smells, and tuberose and gardenia work well for sultry evenings.

3. SCENT FABRICS: Use a lime-scented linen spray on laundered linens, towels, and clothes. This will keep not only clothing, bedding, and towels smelling deliciously fresh but also their storage space. Sandalwood soap, still wrapped, can be placed in bedroom drawers to keep them, and the content, pleasantly scented. Linen sprays are also great for infusing a subtle scent on lingerie and clothes. Lavender-fragranced linen sprays are perfect for giving bed linens a laundered-in-the-fresh-air scent and, when spritzed under pillows before bedtime, encourage a peaceful slumber.

4. SCENTED WATER AND HERBS: Fill decorative bowls with hot water and just add scented bath oil. Fragrance will linger in the air even after the water cools. Fill drawstring bags with fresh lavender, rosemary, and tiny eucalyptus leaves and place behind cushions on the sofa. As soon as someone takes a seat, the bag is crushed, and the scent is released. The same mixture can be used to place in bowls.

Eucalyptus is particularly good as it has a very clean scent and dries naturally.

5. POTPOURRI: To create a welcoming ambience, place large chunky potpourri in open bowls or vases in your hallway or entrance. You can regularly revive the scent of the potpourri by placing it in a plastic bag, dropping in a bit of reviver oil, sealing the bag, and leaving it overnight. Upon opening in the morning, the potpourri pieces will be thoroughly refreshed. Spicy warm notes are great for colder seasons, and fresh citrus and florals are perfect for spring and summer. You can make your own potpourri by lining the bottom of a large bowl with coffee beans and fresh cardamom pods to create a wonderful eau de cologne smell, then throw on ready dried orange slices, cinnamon sticks, fresh kumquats, or cherries.

55

DESIGN A BEDROOM

CELERIE KEMBLE

Celerie Kemble is an interior designer for Kemble Interiors Inc.,

a decorating and design firm located in Palm Beach and

New York. She also designs a self-named line of furniture for

Lane Venture, fabric for Braemore, and wallpaper

for Zoffany. She has been featured as one of House Beautiful

magazine's Top 100 Designers for five consecutive years

and was named one of the fifty tastemakers for the future

of design by House & Garden *magazine.*

A bedroom is our most personal enclave where we are most bare, private, and sensual, or just plain hiding. The challenge is to create physical comfort as well as a functional but aesthetically pleasing space. To make this room special, you must cater to many senses—sight, touch, sound, and smell. I can't tell you how to decorate your room, as that is entirely personal, but I can pass on some advice.

BED

Please indulge yourself here! Fabulous sheets are a bonus but not a necessity. Some designers cry thread count as though it's an anthem, but I believe that pillows, comforter, and mattress have more influence over the entire bed experience. You wouldn't buy a car without test driving it—think of your bed the same way. Go to the showroom and flop around on the mattresses, hug the pillows, and rub the sheets against your cheeks before you make a purchase.

LIGHTING

* An overlit bedroom lacks romance. Make use of dimmers, three-way, and full spectrum and dipped bulbs, which show varying brightness and can direct light in specific directions. Or use lampshades with soft opacity.
* Lighting looks best when at a variety of heights. Aim for four levels of lighting: table, standing, ceiling, and wall mounted. This is gentle on the eyes and combats harsh and unflattering shadows. I recommend using wall-mounted swing arms near the bed (a great trick for smaller bedrooms), a standing lamp, and table lamps on a chest of drawers or bedside tables.
* I think of lighting as jewelry and encourage you to hold out for something you love rather than making a quick purchase. Because they're small, easily stocked, and easily shipped, great lamps are always available in antique shops, flea markets, and online auctions.

WINDOW TREATMENTS

It's one of the only rooms in the house that begs the management of darkness as well as light, so think carefully about your window treatments. In the absence of financial constraints, a perfectly dressed window has a few layers. I like to use hidden but inexpensive blackout shades, sheers, matchstick or wooden blinds, and outer panels or a pretty roman shade. The panels and roman shade are mostly decorative, but they soften a room dramatically and add the illusion of greater height. (I recommend setting the shade, valance, and curtain pole all the way up to the ceiling.)

WALLS

The bedroom is the leading candidate for special wall treatment.

* *Wallpaper:* Consider a good stripe, graphic patterns, and textures.
* *Upholstered walls:* Like living in a jewel box, this expensive option envelopes you with the fabric's texture, pattern, and color.
* *Paint finishes:* The glossier the finish, the easier to clean (good for trim and doors); the more matted the finish, the easier to repaint over smudges. I usually do eggshell walls and semi-gloss or satin on the doors.

FLOORS

Because there is less traffic here, you can use more delicate flooring options.

* I prefer wall-to-wall carpet because of the blanketing, clean, calm effect and the delicious decadence of soft pile beneath bare feet. Also, this floor treatment distinguishes the bedroom from other rooms in the house, which are more likely to have area rugs over flooring.
* If you chose an area rug, remember that your eye is naturally drawn to the perimeter line creating the perception that the room is only as large as the rug. If that doesn't dissuade you, keep in mind that electric cords, dust bunnies, and general household junk tend to accumulate in what I think of as the ghetto between rug and wall.
* If you don't choose carpeting or rugs, paint wood floors white or a

soft color, then accent with throw rugs. Or use a dark stain and keep the furniture light for high contrast.

FURNITURE

While the selection process is personal, here is a list of items to consider: bed, side tables, desk, seating area, chest of drawers, storage, a mirror. I don't like sets and prefer that each piece of furniture relate but not match in a room. For instance, I like to use two coherent but differently styled and scaled bedside tables. One might be closed (to hide books, glasses, etc.) and one more leggy and open, or I'll use a small table on one side and put a writing desk or vanity as a side table on the other.

A secondary seating option is a necessity for a bedroom. It's a matter of manners to make sure there is somewhere for a nonintimate person to sit as there will always be occasions when they are in the room with you. At a minimum, a pull-up chair or bench will do. If space and budget permit, place a small loveseat at the foot of the bed, or a chaise in the corner of a room, or a comfy reading chair and ottoman in a corner.

TIPS AND TREATS

* A tray next to the bed is a pretty and practical way to keep mess minimal and easily portable.
* Treat yourself to an outrageously soft throw blanket at the foot of your bed.
* For storage, think big Tupperware under your bed. Put your stuff in the large, flat plastic containers. They keep everything from getting dusty and they are easy to access.
* Put a surge protector or extension cord under each side of the bed. This saves you from crawling under the bed and tugging the plug off the wall. Always tape cords down the back legs of furniture so they're not snaking around in view.

56

CHOOSE A COLOR

CHRISTOPHER LOWELL

Christopher Lowell is host of the Emmy-winning Christopher Lowell Show *on the Discovery Home Channel. He is the creator of the Christopher Lowell Home Collection and the author of several books, including* Christopher Lowell's Seven Layers of Design: Fearless, Fabulous Decorating.

Even though we see in color, dress in color, and are surrounded by color every day, putting it up on our walls is a commitment we find hard to make. Yet we'll spend thousands of dollars on everything else in the room hoping for warmth and character—in order to avoid the wall color issue. Why? Well, in my experience, it's actually not about choosing color. It's just paint. If you hate it, you paint over it . . . no big whoop. The reality is it's about confronting the fear of choice itself. Paint color is abstract and subjective. It's the psychological way you prepare yourself to introduce color into your home that will ensure you'll be happy with your choice. Here's how:

1. UNDERSTAND THAT COLOR IS THE FIRST LAYER OF DECORATION IN THE ROOM AND THAT THERE ARE SEVEN MORE LAYERS TO COME. So by the time you add carpet, upholstery, accent fabric, nonupholstered furniture, accessories, and wall art, then plants and lighting, how much of that color are you really going to see? It will simply peek out around the bookcase, from behind the sofa, at the baseboard. So remember what you're choosing is not an accent color, but a *background color*. You're looking for a color that has a deep, warm, dusty value to it—a color that will surround all the things in the room and tie them together. If you're stuck for colors you love, check out your wardrobe. Eliminate the black-and-white clothing and see the colors you wear most. Chances are if it looks good *on* you, it will look good *around* you.

2. NEVER CHOOSE A COLOR AT THE PAINT STORE! If you're dieting, you should never grocery shop when you're hungry, and this is no different. Don't try to make the critical choice in an atmosphere of intimidation and chaos. Besides, don't you think it would be a good idea to actually look at the swatch in question in the room it's actually being considered for?

3. NEVER BRING HOME PAINT ON YOUR FIRST STORE VISIT. It's the swatches you want to bring home first. Not just one, but as many as you think you might want to consider—that's what they're there for so don't be shy.

4. PUT THE SWATCHES IN THE ROOM YOU'RE CONSIDERING THEM FOR ON A SURFACE IN A HIGH-TRAFFIC AREA. Give yourself a week of walking by them every day. On the first day you'll eliminate about half of them, wondering, "What was I thinking?" And remember, when in

doubt, go darker, because by the time it's up on the walls, it will appear at least two shades lighter. Your mission is to choose three colors—one for the walls, one for the trim, and yes, one for the ceiling too. By leaving it white, you might as well spread a bedsheet over it and declare it unfinished. If you're feeling insecure, find a paint strip you like. On it will be at least four to five shades from lightest to darkest—all derivations of the came color. Choose the very lightest for your trim, the third to the lightest for your ceiling, and the medium-dark shade for the walls. You'll find that over the course of the week, you'll make your own natural process of elimination work for you.

5. STICK TO YOUR GUNS. When you get back to Testosterone City (the building supply store), don't chicken out—buy the color you chose at home, even when "Bob" pops off the lid and you gasp!

6. DON'T PANIC. When you roll the first stroke of color onto the wall, you'll have a stroke, too. We all second-guess ourselves. Don't make a judgment about your choice until all references of white are gone. Turn the light off and go to bed. When you wake up, the light will be streaming in, your mind-set will have changed, and all will be well with the world and your walls.

57

PAINT A LIVING ROOM

Bonnie Rosser Krims

Bonnie Rosser Krims is a nationally recognized architectural

paint color expert and author of four books, including

Perfect Palettes for Painting Rooms.

The largest "canvas" in the living room is its walls. With paint, we change not only the color of the walls but also the mood of the room.

How should your living room feel—uplifting, calm, serene? I tend to ignore advice that says cool colors make you feel tranquil and warm colors make you feel cheerful. Choose colors that make you feel good.

GET STARTED

Take your color cues from an existing object in the living room and use that as a point of departure. This might be a favorite rug, pillow, or drapes. Isolate colors that you like from that object. After you have settled on swatches, you may choose to test the color on the wall.

TEST YOUR LIVING ROOM PAINT COLORS

1. Test the color on a section of white wall for an accurate assessment. If the wall isn't white, apply primer to your test section.
2. Use a 3-inch disposable foam brush to paint a 2×2-foot test swatch on a window wall, usually the darkest wall in the room, and another on the opposite wall.
3. Wait 20 minutes and apply another coat. Dark paint colors may require 3 coats.
4. Place objects from the room, like pillows, near or against your dried test swatch to evaluate the color in context.
5. Look at the sample over several days. See how the color appears at different times of day. If the color doesn't truly appeal to you, don't use it. Test another color.
6. Test your ceiling and trim colors as well.

Create even more character in the room by painting the ceiling. Pale blue on the ceiling evokes the sky. Soft yellow suggests sunlight. Or try taking 1 cup of the wall color and pouring it into white ceiling paint. It will gently tint the ceiling color, creating a link with the wall color. Trim is typically painted white or off-white, but you can enhance the room further by using colored trim.

PAINT THE LIVING ROOM

The most commonly used wall paint is latex, a water-based paint that is easy to clean up. Use an eggshell, satin, or low-luster finish. The name of the finish varies from one paint company to the next. All are more reflective and durable than flat paint.

1. Clean walls and trim with an ammonia/water solution.
2. Fill small holes using a putty knife and spackle. Sand when dry. Prime these areas.

3. Paint the ceiling. Using ceiling paint and a 2-inch brush, paint the ceiling where it meets the walls and trim ("cutting in"). Roll paint on the remaining area.

4. Paint the walls. Cut in using a 2-inch brush along the top of the wall/ceiling edge. Cut in around the windows and doors and other woodwork.

5. Roll walls with a ¼-inch smooth or ⅜-inch semi-smooth roller cover. Start at the top of the wall and work downward.

6. Paint the trim (window frames, sashes, doors, woodwork) using a semi-gloss paint (slightly glossy, durable, easy to wash finish) and a 1–2½-inch wide-angled edge brush.

Save any leftover paint for touch-ups.

A FEW FOOLPROOF COLORS

Benjamin Moore	Citrus Mist 141 (pale apricot/yellow)
Pratt and Lambert	Caramel Tint 2087 (warm golden yellow)
Martha Stewart	Salmon Faverolle (complex off-white; creates atmosphere without much color)
Benjamin Moore	Soft Fern 2144-40 (delicate, serene green)
Pittsburgh Paints	Fountain Mist 405-1 (pastel blue)
Benjamin Moore	Pumpkin Pie 2167-20 (striking orange/gray)
California Paints	Portsmouth Spice (rich, bold rust/red)

For trim, I favor Benjamin Moore White Dove (a nonyellowing white).

58

LIGHT A ROOM

DEBBIE TRAVIS

Debbie Travis is the author of eight best-selling books on decorating and design based on her award-winning television shows, Debbie Travis' The Painted House *and* Debbie Travis' Facelift. *Travis's weekly syndicated newspaper column,* House to Home, *appears across the United States and Canada.*

When making plans to decorate a room, the process usually begins with thoughts of color schemes and furniture placement. I have long touted the magical transformation a coat of paint can perform on any room, but without proper lighting a room cannot function well. Good lighting is essential to any decorating scheme. It gives life to the color on the walls and brings out the textures and shapes in fabric and furnishings. Poor lighting can be visually stressful, while a room that has been well lit contributes to a feeling of comfort and ease.

Rooms are seldom perfect. A well-executed lighting scheme will allow you to camouflage or downplay the faults and highlight the best features. Lighting can change the feeling of space.

By flooding a wall with up lighting, a small room feels more spacious, while table lamps and the warm light radiating from a fireplace bring a cozy, familiar glow to a large room.

Think about how you will be using your room, and then choose from the following lighting categories to complement the way the space functions as well as how it looks and feels.

NATURAL LIGHT

If you have large windows or skylights, take full advantage of the welcoming light throughout the day. Light affects the way we see color and intense sunlight makes a dramatic difference by turning even the darkest colors pale. The movement of natural light produces intriguing shadows and patterns that become part of the room's architecture.

AMBIENT LIGHT

This encompassing light includes natural light, but its effect is more commonly felt after dark. Plan for the ambient light to be bright and fill the room. You can build up this effect by combining different light sources, and control the room's ambience with dimmers. Ceiling fixtures shed light downward, wall sconces can be directed up and down, and floor and table lamps create pools of light.

ACCENT LIGHTING

Choose accent lighting to accentuate your favorite objects or interesting architectural features. Art and photo lights, shelf lights for glass-front cabinets and interesting open storage units, and up lights for plants and wall washing are designed for this purpose. Accent lighting is a great tool for steering attention away from less attractive parts of the room and allows you to build on the character and atmosphere you would like to promote.

TASK LIGHTING

When you are reading, working at a hobby, cooking, or serving dinner, proper lighting is most important. This form of light should shine directly over the work surface so that you can see without straining your eyes. The best task lights have reflectors that can be adjusted to cast light where it is needed.

DECORATIVE LIGHTING

These are lamps or chandeliers that are chosen for their fabulous or funky design appeal rather than as a light source. A decorative light can be one of the key features in your room's décor, and is not meant to illuminate anything on a serious level. Leave that to your ambient and task lighting.

KINETIC LIGHTING

Kinetic lighting is all about movement—the dancing flames in a fireplace and flickering candlelight are the most basic examples. Retro Lava lamps and revolving spotlights are meant to create atmosphere and are for fun.

Good lighting for your home does not have to be an expensive proposition. Use your imagination and make a plan employing these key elements as a guide. Let the huge variety of lighting products available inspire you to light your rooms brilliantly.

59

HANG WALLPAPER

Susan Sargent

Susan Sargent is an artist, textile designer, and author.
Her coordinating wallpaper, fabrics, rugs, and paints
are sold through her two stores and on her website. Her
latest book is The Comfort of Color.

I have been painting with vivid colors since I could hold a brush, but wallpaper was always a no-go zone. The mystery of how to hang it inhabited a Three Stooges moment: a backward fall off a ladder, wrapped in yards of soggy and vindictive wallpaper. Available patterns leaned heavily toward the traditional, the drab, and the precious. Today, new designs and new ideas for mixing and matching patterns and borders have made wallpaper fun again. It's a simple way to add interest, texture, and color to rooms, and prepasted papers are easy to install and maintain.

CHOOSING WALLPAPER

There are endless varieties, available at do-it-yourself stores, through decorator showrooms, or in many hardware stores. Traditional florals, glittery novelty prints, embossed vinyls, velvets, suedes, and traditional reproductions are all available. Here is how to select one that's right for your home:

1. *Color and Pattern:* Choose an overall color that will work well with your furnishings. If you have many floral fabrics on the living room upholstery, consider stripes or a tone-on-tone pattern. If your upholstery is neutral, make a splash with a bold color and design.
2. *Scale:* Don't overwhelm a small room with a large-scale pattern or, conversely, use a tiny print in a large room.
3. *Variations:* Consider using different patterns for different walls. Wallpaper can be combined with painted walls. Wallpaper can be used on a ceiling. Use borders at either ceiling height or chair-rail height.
4. *Durability:* Take into consideration the location and usage. High-traffic areas (kids' rooms, hallways, kitchens) should have correspondingly durable papers. Papers range from the lightly washable to the quasi-industrial (e.g., vinyl).
5. *Convenience:* Most wallpapers are prepasted for easier installation. Wallpaper is also easier to remove than it used to be—so don't feel you're locked in to it for life.

HANGING WALLPAPER

Here are ten easy tips for hanging your own wallpaper:

1. *Order enough paper.* Measure each wall and calculate the square footage. Deduct for doors and windows. Order 30–40 percent more than you think you'll need.
2. *Smooth walls.* Remove old paper or loose paint and sand the walls. Every bump or ridge will show up under the new papers.

3. *Prime.* Size walls with a brush or roller to avoid bubbles and to make it easier to position.

4. *Start straight.* Use a plumb line and level to get your first edge perfectly straight. This is possibly your most critical step.

5. *Preplan.* Plan ahead to avoid ending up with a squirrelly little piece at the last corner. Orient the pattern in relation to the ceiling.

6. *Cut.* Cut the first strip using a metal straightedge. Leave about 2 extra inches, top and bottom, for trimming. Near corners, leave a half-inch overlap.

7. *Book.* On a large table, covered with a drop cloth, wet the paper. For unpasted wallpaper, use a paint roller or wide brush to apply paste. For prepasted wallpaper, use a water tray to submerge the rolled paper. Soak for the recommended amount of time. Fold the damp top half down to the middle and then fold the bottom up to the middle, paste to paste. Gently roll. Let sit 3–5 minutes. This allows the adhesive to activate, and the paper to relax.

8. *Hang.* Unfold top half and position paper at ceiling. Slide into position to align with the plumb line. Smooth out. Do not stretch. Unfold bottom half. Smooth the whole strip, working diagonally from the top down and from the center outward. Get rid of any air bubbles or creases.

9. *Trim.* Use a wall scraper as a guide and trim the excess paper with a sharp razor knife.

10. *Finish.* Wash off excess paste with a clean, damp sponge.

60

SELECT WINDOW TREATMENTS

CHARLES RANDALL

Charles Randall is the best-selling author of The Encyclopedia
of Window Fashions. *He has decorated over 60,000 windows.*

The two most important considerations to keep in mind when
deciding on a window treatment are function and style. Knowing
what you need your window treatment to do for you and being
aware of what kind of feel you want it to impart will allow you
more focus when making your purchase.

FUNCTION

First, decide what role you want the window treatment to play in
the room. Will it be purely for the aesthetic enhancement of your
home, or do you need it for a more practical purpose such as creating privacy or blocking out sunlight? Are you trying to draw
attention to a fabulous view or to hide the spectacle of the
unsightly home across the street?

Create a list of the most important features your window
treatment should have. This will influence which types of window treatments may be appropriate. If you have small children,
you probably do not want mini-blinds with long cords that can
pose a safety hazard or draperies in rich silks that can become

quickly damaged. If you care more about the ornamental value of a window treatment, however, a drapery made of silk fabrics that puddle on the floor may be perfect for you. For privacy, roman shades or wooden shutters paired with draperies are both excellent solutions.

STYLE

Once the more practical aspects of window dressing are dealt with you can begin the fun part: using your creativity to embellish your home. Although you needn't stick with a time period or theme when decorating, it is important to make sure that your window treatment will complement the existing features of your home and furnishings.

Think about the mood you are trying to achieve. If you want your home office to appear chic and modern, go with simple lines and minimal detail. Two superb options here are blinds and shades. Both are relatively easy to maintain, needing only a little dusting, and provide a professional look that will not be overly distracting. The cost can be as little as $20 for aluminum blinds and as much as $300 or more for wood blinds, while shades range in price from $50 for simple roller shades to $300 and up for sheer verticals.

If you want your bedroom to appear sumptuous and exude warmth, use luxurious textiles, layered in rich tones. Draperies are a more expensive option than blinds or shades, with an unlimited range of prices depending on the fabrics used, the intricacy of design, and the size of the window. They can be somewhat difficult to maintain because of the delicate nature of fabric, and they collect dust, but draperies provide a cozy and inviting look that, for many, is worth the cost and effort.

Window treatments can also be used to disguise flaws in a room, or to accent its features. If your living room has only a tiny window, you can make it appear larger by hanging your draperies higher than usual and using more fabric to accent its sides. If a room is lacking texture or warmth, you can introduce these elements by choosing opulent fabrics or vivid hues. If you want to display a stunning ocean view, keep the window treatment simple yet elegant to draw the eye to the outside.

Most important, stay true to your own personal style while being realistic about how your window treatment will perform inside your home.

Avoid these common mistakes:

* Never put mini-blinds over a sliding glass door. Because of the height of these windows, the strings become too long once the blinds are pulled up. The blinds may stack so thickly at the top of the windows that you will bump your head passing through the doors.
* Never use a fabric tape measure or attempt to "eye-ball" a window's size. Always use a steel tape measure to take your windows' measurements.
* Don't forget to consider whether your window treatment will be visible from another room, and to account for that when choosing colors, textures, and shapes.
* Don't try to do it all yourself. Consult a professional.

61

BUY ART

BARBARA GUGGENHEIM

Barbara Guggenheim has been a leading art consultant for the

past twenty-five years. As a partner in Guggenheim Asher

Associates, she has built art collections for some of the country's

top corporations and numerous individuals.

You've got a sofa with a big, blank wall behind it. Or you've moved to a new house or apartment with lots of empty wall space. Either way, you need a painting.

Buying your first piece of art can be a downright daunting task. The stark white art galleries are intimidating, and there are so many of them that it's hard to know where to begin. Worse, it's hard to make a judgment call and tell good from bad art. And, finally, there's the question of how much to pay. Below are some steps you can take to ensure a prudent purchase:

1. LOOK AT ART MAGAZINES AND AUCTION CATALOGS. Going to galleries and auctions is also helpful. Art fairs, where hundreds of dealers bring works, are like taking a crash course, as they offer a quick way of seeing thousands of works of art at one time. Following the fairs is like making a pilgrimage to a

holy site. You'll be exposed to a wide range of styles and areas from which you can choose, and you'll get a feel for prices.

2. TAKE YOUR TIME. Acclimating to the new trends and learning how the art market works takes time.

3. ASK QUESTIONS. When you see something you like in a gallery, don't be afraid to ask about it. Even if you have to ask the name of the artist, don't be shy. How will you ever learn if you don't start by asking questions? In addition to issues such as how a piece of art is made or what an artist is doing, ask what museums or private collections own or have shown the work.

4. GET THE RIGHT ADVICE. You wouldn't drill an oil well without consulting geologists, would you? Nor would you buy a business without getting a lawyer's advice. Buying a painting should be no different. Don't think that you can make wise decisions without the benefit of expertise. Local museum curators and art advisors can be a great help.

5. BUY WITH YOUR EYES, NOT YOUR EARS. Don't buy something just because someone has told you it's a good investment. You should be able to find a piece you love that has the possibility of increasing in value too.

6. DON'T FEEL YOU HAVE TO PLUNGE IN AND BUY SOMETHING EXPENSIVE. Get your feet wet by buying less expensive works, such as drawings or photos. Later, you'll learn that buying good art isn't spending money. It's merely converting it from one investment instrument to another. Still, you have to be careful: too often newcomers make the mistake of buying "names" without considering the quality of the work.

7. EXERCISE DUE DILIGENCE. Check prices on Artnet, a service that lists prior auction records for the artist. Call other galleries and see what other works by the artist are or have been on the market recently. Have the condition checked by an independent restorer and make certain, if it is an old painting, that IFAR (The International Foundation for Art Research) shows no record of its being stolen at IFAR. And make sure the reigning expert on the artist has acknowledged the authenticity of the work.

8. MAKE AN OFFER ACCORDINGLY. Factor in prior auction records and other recent sales, rarity, and other complexities.

9. GO FOR THE BURN. Traditionally, the paintings that go up the most in value are those that are among the artist's best, so stretch and get only the "A" works by an artist—even if it hurts!

10. INSURE YOUR INVESTMENT. Once you've paid for the piece, have it insured. Install the work (securely) and enjoy it! If you lend it to an exhibition, make sure there's adequate security. I sleep better when I know that a painting is under shatterproof UV-filtered glass with a strong backing.

62

GROW A FLOWER

REBECCA KOLLS

Rebecca Kolls is the host of a nationally syndicated TV show,
Rebecca's Garden, *and the gardening and lifestyle contributor*
for ABC's Good Morning America. *She is the author of*
Rebecca's Garden: Four Seasons to Grow On.

Let's start with a flower you can't kill—hemerocallis. Just the complicated name alone sounds ominous, but don't let it fool you. This perennial is anything but! Commonly known as the daylily, this is a plant for the novice gardener. Daylilies are one of America's most popular perennials. Their soft, delicate beauty belies their undemanding toughness. Unlike most flowers, daylilies thrive on neglect with respect. They can take a beating for sure, they are drought tolerant, and rarely have a run-in with disease and pests—all while providing you with lovely flowers, sometimes adding up to fifty a day! And as the name implies, the flowers do only last a day but are quickly replaced with new buds.

Daylilies come in an array of colors mainly in the pastel palette. Flowers are circular, triangular, and star-shaped. And not all blooms are created equal in size—some are fewer than

3 inches wide, while the larger versions will open their faces beyond 5 inches. Their pretty petals can be small and smooth, fancy and ruffled, or stately and rigid. And to top it off, some daylilies give a command performance—meaning they will bloom twice a season.

The height of these plants varies as much as their color and shape. If you need a small, front-of-the-border plant growing about a foot tall, you'll find it. Or if it's a vertical focal point you're searching for, some daylilies climb 4 feet and higher.

CLIMATE

Daylilies can be grown almost anywhere in the country. When purchasing your prized plant, look for one that has healthy green foliage and lots of buds. They appreciate a sunny location and are not fussy about the soils, but if you really want to start them off on the right foot, prepare their new home by mixing in compost, rotted manure, and peat moss.

PLANTING

Planting is a piece of cake, simply dig a hole as deep as the container and twice as wide. Gently remove the flower from its container. If the roots are wound together (many perennials are), take a sharp knife and cut an X through the bottom and score the sides of the plant a few times around the perimeter. Gently loosen the roots and place the daylily in the hole. Gently pack the soil around the plant and water well.

Daylilies don't require any additional babysitting so sit back and relax. Be sure to water when rain isn't in the forecast—but don't overdo it. And when temperatures heat up under the summer sun, add a 3–4-inch layer of mulch around the base of the plant. This will help retain moisture while keeping the weeds out.

One word of caution. If you plan on cutting blooms to enjoy indoors, you need to cut out the stamens of the flower (the stringy stalks protruding from the center) with a pair of scissors. They hold lots of yellow pollen that stains anything it touches. To keep your daylilies looking terrific year after year, you need to divide them. That means, every 3–5 years dig up the plant after it blooms, cut it into 3 chunks, and replant. This is a great way to get additional plants for free while expanding your blooming power.

Now you have a flowering plant that's virtually indestructible.

63

DESIGN A BATHROOM

NANCY EPSTEIN

Nancy Epstein is founder and CEO of Artistic Tile,

an industry leader in luxury stone, artisan tile, distinctive

fittings, and home accessories.

The bath is the most personal room in the home, so don't resist the urge to design a room you'll love. Any color or style done in good taste will add to the resale value of your home.

TILE

Start the design with the element you see the most of—tile. If you have a color you've always loved, you'll continue to love it, so use it. You'll also want to explore the diversity of materials and finishes on the market. Fortunately, there are thousands of suitable products.

* *Porcelain tile:* Often designed to mimic stone or terra-cotta, porcelain is durable and stain resistant.
* *Ceramic tile:* If you love color, you'll find myriad choices here.
* *Stone:* Stone should last as long as the pyramids. I refuse to differentiate among marble, limestone, granite, and slate, as it would be a very rare stone that when properly sealed by the

installer would not be suitable for a residential bathroom. Different finishes of natural stone (polished, honed, tumbled) will create various looks.

* *Glass:* Easy to care for and impervious, it is no wonder the Romans loved using glass in mosaics. On the floor, however, large sizes get slippery, so beware.
* *Terra-cotta:* Most real terra-cotta develops issues with constant exposure to water, so save it for your kitchen or use a porcelain substitute.

DETAILS

Plan decorative tile details (mosaic borders, 3-D moldings, etc.) at focal points. Avoid using details where electrical outlets and shower valves will interrupt the design. Also consider the following:

* *The mirror:* Your mirror over the sink is the artwork of your bathroom, so whatever your budget, be sure this area is beautifully done.
* *Chair rail:* In the bath, this is the height between the vanity countertop and the mirror or medicine cabinet.
* *Shower:* Another highly visible spot is the main shower wall. Consider adding a framed panel with textured tile, or a contrasting pattern or color in the center. The frame can be made with ceramic, glass, or stone moldings that match or complement the tile.

PLUMBING FIXTURES

If you think of tile as the clothing of the bath and faucetry and fixtures as the jewelry and accessories, having selected your tile first will ease your aesthetic plumbing decisions. Some practical considerations:

* *Handheld shower fixture:* Consider a hand shower on a sliding bar in addition to your main showerhead. It makes short work of clean-

ing your shower, tub, child, or pet, and ladies can shower without
disturbing coiffed hair.

* *Faucet height:* Be certain that the height of your faucet won't interfere with opening your medicine cabinet.
* *Sinks:* Look for sinks in interesting materials such as metal, glass,
or stone for texture. Undermount the sink to free up counter space.
* *Vanities:* When choosing a vanity, consider your storage needs. A
pedestal sink may be elegant, but if you choose one, plan to add a
separate cabinet.

LIGHTING

Lighting is as important a consideration in your bathroom as it is in
other rooms of your house. Think about the following:

* *No squinting:* Plan appropriate task light, and don't forget a light in
the shower.
* *Skylights:* Skylights are great for bringing in natural light. Tile
them inside to prevent damage from condensation or humidity.

MAKING A SMALL BATHROOM APPEAR LARGER

If you can't change the size of your bathroom, here are some tips to
make it appear larger than it is:

* *Shape:* Surprisingly, shape and pattern can make a room appear
vastly larger or smaller. Rather than lined-up square tiles, try rectangular brick shapes or lay squares diagonally on the diamond to
increase visual width.
* *Scale:* Small tile actually makes a room look smaller, while large tile
makes a room appear larger.
* *Transparency:* Install a frameless glass shower door. A curtain
divides the room, while clear glass opens it up.

INSTALLATION: GIVE AN EXPERT THE LAST WORD

Even beautiful, quality products can disappoint (and may not work properly or pass building inspections) unless professionally installed. Plumbers and electricians must be licensed and, for tile installers, get references from someone whose aesthetic you trust.

64

ARRANGE FURNITURE

Nina Campbell

Nina Campbell is an interior designer and author of three books,
including Nina Campbell's Decorating Notebook: Insider
Secrets and Decorating Ideas for Your Home. *She has two*
retail outlets in London, and her fabric, carpet, paint, and
wallpaper collections are distributed worldwide.

The first thing to do when designing your room is to work out
what you want from the room. Think about how many people
you are going to need to seat. Is this is a room where you are
going to watch television or sleep? Do you want to have an area
for a dining table and chairs?

DRAWING A FLOOR PLAN

The most common mistakes have to do with scale. The furniture
is often either too large or too small. For example, a large sofa
and two small chairs would seem unbalanced. Or there is too
much of it or not enough (at least this means you've got a shopping opportunity!). I find that it is vital to have a floor plan to get
the scale of the room. I suggest using a half inch to represent a
foot; then, with a scale rule, you can measure and draw your

furniture onto the plan. Alternatively, when you have decided what pieces of furniture you want, make cutouts to scale of these pieces of furniture and rearrange them on your empty floor plan. This can show you, for example, if your sofa is too deep and will therefore overwhelm a room and will save you from making huge and expensive mistakes when buying furniture.

WHERE TO PUT EVERYTHING

The living room makes the biggest impact so it is a good place to start. Deciding where to put everything is important because if a furniture layout gets out of hand, it can resemble a knitting circle. If you have a fireplace, this should be the natural focus to the sitting area. If you don't, this could be a place to put a unit or a cabinet with a television, books, and objects.

The classic furniture arrangement is either sofas opposite each other or one sofa with a pair of easy chairs opposite. Always choose comfortable sofas, and make sure that your furniture is not necessarily all the same height, as this can make the room look like a furniture

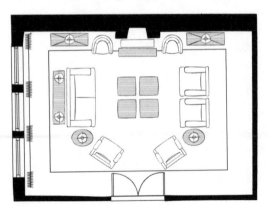

showroom. If I am working with a fireplace, I like to flank it with two small occasional chairs as this gives a nice talking group and looks inviting. I would also consider bringing in a pair of elbow chairs as this makes a perfect sitting group of eight, and with the addition of a couple of stools in front of the fireplace, you can even add another two people. Make sure you leave enough room to enter your sitting area and circulate within it. Allow a 3-foot gap for moving around—this accommodates most people.

If you want a television in this room, maybe have bookcases or cabinets on either side of the fireplace and put a television in one of them. Depending on the size of your television and the height of your sofa and armchairs, test how far away from it you place your furniture so that you can watch comfortably. These bookcases can also be a nice source of design when used to place photographs, objects, and books (of course) and can even be used to contain lamps or other forms of lighting.

If you are going to have people over for drinks, think about where you are going to be able to put hors d'oeuvres. The stool in front of the fireplace could be used for this if it isn't already used for a guest. Additionally, make sure that occasional tables are arranged so that each guest has a place to put down his or her drink.

Take a long time planning a room and, once it is done, relax and enjoy it. Your room will work much better if you are confident in it.

65

RENOVATE A KITCHEN

Fu-Tung Cheng

Fu-Tung Cheng is principal of award-winning Cheng Design,

located in Berkeley, California. He is the author of Concrete at

Home *and the best-selling* Concrete Countertops.

Sit down with a glass of wine and calculate how much you could bear to spend on the kitchen. Double it and add another 20 percent. Realistically, that's how much you *will* spend even if you are disciplined and manage the deluge of desires to come.

The good news is that all that money spent on the development of a well-designed kitchen is better than money in the bank. Once finished, not only will you enjoy the fruits of your labor, but should you move, the kitchen will inevitably be the selling point of the house and you will most likely recoup everything you spent with sizable interest to boot! That's why I advise you to build whatever you can possibly afford within reason.

I have never seen a case in which someone regretted spending too much on their kitchen renovation. Traditionally, no matter the cost or the location, people have on average spent 15–35 percent of the *market value* of their home (including land) on remodeling kitchens. Over time, everything gets astronomically more expensive, so do it right, do it all, do it now.

"Do it right" means good planning, good design, good craftsmanship, and good bang for your buck. Research the myriad kitchen design books and magazines to determine a space that feels good to you. Study the material choices and configurations. Good planning means preparing for a period of 4 to 24 weeks of constant disruption.

Visualize your friends and relatives picking at your culinary creations while you are prepping their meal. Do you want them there? Or would you rather herd them as far away as possible? This exercise will indicate if you prefer an open plan, where guests mingle with the chef, or a closed one where they are kept from intruding with a dividing counter.

Kitchens are the gathering place, watering hole, feeding trough, and traffic hub of the modern home. Traffic and circulation patterns with adjacent spaces and rooms should flow around and along edges of the kitchen and/or specific counters, like islands, so that community is encouraged without interfering with cooking and washing activities. Space permitting, it is always nice to have a walk-in food pantry and a smaller food-prep sink with a wood chopping board, separate from a larger dish/cleaning sink. It's wise to plan for recycling and compost bins, bulletin-board, small office area, and a small TV if so desired.

Good design can mean different things to different people. For me, it means cutting-edge, timeless design, design that relies as much on emotion as it does on form and function. Emotion emerges from the space, the light, and the form—the architecture, the structure, and the "bones" of the design, which are flushed out with craftsmanship and materials. Sometimes it means building in *inefficiency.*

Think of those old brick ovens and tile counters in a kitchen in Provence, France, with little or no cabinetry and a simple spigot over a stone sink, or imagine the simple elegance of a farmhouse in Japan. Try to steer away from cramming every possible function, appliance, and device into the room. Avoid cookie-cutter designs of relentless wood box-style base cabinets topped with thin countertops and an array of wall cabinets. Avoid flashy colors.

You may have to seek professional help. Architects, if they are cooks themselves, can create beautiful and functional kitchens. Independent kitchen designers can also help the process. Check out portfolios of past work and call references.

Cabinetry is going to be the one area where you have plenty of leeway to save money by simply doing with less. A kitchen with open shelving in place of wall cabinets is inherently more open, warm, and inviting, and considerably less expensive.

And, of course, you can do it all or partially yourself. If you have more time than money—like I did thirty years ago—then don't hesitate. With simple power tools you can install prefinished flooring and ready-to-assemble cabinets, tile your walls, and pour your own concrete countertops. Savor the moment (months, years), roll up your sleeves, and have some fun. Finish with another glass of wine.

66

STAIN FURNITURE

STEVE SHANESY

Steve Shanesy is the editor and publisher of
Popular Woodworking *magazine.*

Coloring wood furniture with stain can produce beautiful results or a frustrating mess. One thing is guaranteed: it's never as simple as following the directions on the stain product's label or as easy as portrayed in TV ads, but then real life rarely is. A basic understanding of wood, how to prepare the wood surface before staining, and how to apply the stain itself will head off disastrous results.

Wood fibers are a lot like a handful of soda straws. The ends of the straws easily take up liquids while the sides can't suck up liquids at all. The ends of boards are like the open ends of straws. If you apply even a light-colored stain, the end of the board will turn very dark due to the ends sucking up the stain. The same stain applied to the long surfaces of a board will produce a much lighter color. That said, unfortunately many wood species commonly used in furniture have wood fibers that don't run straight like the straws in your hand. When stain is applied, you get an ugly blotched color with very dark areas surrounded by the stain color you had expected.

You can expect all soft woods—pine, fir, and so on—and many light-colored hardwoods—maple, birch, poplar, and even cherry—to blotch when stain is applied. While manufacturers can color these woods without blotching, there are ways even the rank amateur can avoid stain blotching, and I'll clue you in to the secret a bit later.

PREPARATION

Regardless of the wood type, preparing the wood surface to accept the stain is vital. This is true for previously unfinished wood or refinishing. When refinishing, be certain all old finish is removed as well as most of the original stain color. Before sanding, carefully inspect the wood to identify scratches, dents, or glue that may be on the surface. With dents and scratches, stain will collect and result in a darker color, calling attention to the defect. Glue, on the other hand, seals the wood and prevents the stain from coloring. Light scratches can be sanded out, but little can be done about deep scratches, especially in thin veneer. A dent can be "steamed out" by applying a hot clothes iron and a clean, damp rag to the dent. Steaming swells the crushed wood fibers back to their original, plump condition. Errant glue can be sanded away to bare wood.

SANDING

Sanding can be done by hand or, more easily, with a random orbit sander. Progressing from courser to finer grit sandpaper removes the sanding scratches left by the previous, coarser grit. Start with medium-grit 120 sandpaper, followed by 150 grit, and 180 grit for softwoods. Hardwoods should be completed with 220 grit. If sanding by hand, always sand in the direction the grain runs, typically end to end. If using a random orbit sander, sand in any direction.

When done, apply stain after removing the sanding dust from the wood surface.

STAINING

When selecting a stain color, you'll often find color samples at the store. These samples are only a guideline. Colors will be lighter or darker depending on the color of bare wood to which it's applied, how absorbent it is, and how thoroughly you wipe off excess stain.

Most stains must be thoroughly stirred before use. If working on a large project, stir during use. A better stain choice, and the secret to avoiding, although not totally preventing, blotching, is a "gel" stain. A gel stain is just that, a thicker, viscous material that lies on top of the wood rather than soaks in. If you are unsure of the wood species, a gel stain will provide a good measure of insurance against the heartaches of blotchy wood color.

Apply either regular or gel stain with a clean rag, preferably one that is lint-free. Use sufficient stain to achieve a consistent color and allow it a few minutes to penetrate the wood surface. Then wipe off all excess stain using a clean rag. The final wipe should follow the direction of the grain. Aggressive wiping will remove more color. A second application of stain will only add slightly more color.

FINISH

After the stain has completely dried—an instruction on the product label you can rely on—you'll need to apply a protective, clear finish such as varnish, polyurethane, or shellac. Usually, a couple of coats are necessary.

67

CLEAN JEWELRY

Jacob Arabo

Jacob Arabo, aka Jacob the Jeweler, is the founder of
Jacob & Co. His flagship store is located in New York City.

When most people acquire fine jewelry, they intend to keep it for the rest of their lives. Most likely, they will not go to their jeweler every time their diamond rings need a little sparkle or their pearl earrings are looking a little dull. What I tell my customers (and what many have taught me over the years) is that the majority of maintenance, simple cleaning, and shining can be done at home with simple, inexpensive, and easy-to-find household products. Here are my tips:

DIAMONDS

STORAGE

Diamonds are very strong stones and they can scratch and damage other stones (even other diamonds they rub against). Always store each piece of diamond jewelry separately in lint-free cloth or, even better, satin pouches to prevent scratching. These cloths are the same kind you would use to polish your silver. They are inexpensive, handy, and available at any jewelry store.

CLEANING

First, make a slightly soapy bath of warm water and soap (dishwashing liquid is fine). Let the diamond sit in the bath for a few minutes and then take a soft, small-bristled brush, such as a woman's eyebrow brush or children's soft toothbrush, and gently brush the jewelry. Rinse it under warm running water and dry it with a soft, lint-free cloth. Apply gentle pressure while brushing. You can also use this method with ammonia (which is what a professional jewelry-cleaning kit uses) and water. I would use about 80 percent water because the ammonia is so strong. Toothpaste also works well. Put a very small amount of generic toothpaste (even baking soda is okay) on the brush and gently clean. Rinse by running under warm water and pat dry with a lint-free cloth.

Another tip that my wife, Angela, uses frequently is soaking her diamond ring in hot water for about 20 minutes to remove hand cream residue. Soaking your ring in hot (not boiling) water will loosen the grease and oil residue. Once you remove it from the water, give it a quick run under a warm water stream and dry with the soft, lint-free cloth.

The steps I have listed above can be applied to most pieces of jewelry, with the following three exceptions:

EMERALDS

Emeralds are porous stones. This means they are generally softer than other stones and need to be treated more sensitively. When you want to clean a piece of jewelry that features emeralds, rub it first with a tissue to get the top layer of dirt off, then gently rub it with a Q-tip dipped in warm soapy water, and then polish it dry with a soft, lint-free cloth.

PEARLS

The better you treat your pearls, the longer they will last without discoloring. Do not expose your pearls to perfume, makeup, or sweat. When pearls are looking dull, gently wipe them with a slightly damp jewelry cloth (as described above). Let them dry completely before wearing them again or putting back in the jewelry pouch. If pearls are strung on natural fiber, they should be restrung professionally once a year because the string will break down over time and collect the dirt from a year's worth of wear. If the pearls are strung on an artificial string, have them professionally cleaned once every two years. Do not use hot water or a steamer on pearls.

WATCHES

Do not attempt to clean your watch at home! If you think that dirt, dust, lint, grease, lotion, or anything along these lines has gotten into your watch, take it to a professional for cleaning and a checkup. Most watches come with a warranty—save it and use it.

68

DECORATE WITH FLOWERS

PRESTON BAILEY

*Preston Bailey is the florist to the stars. He has used his
signature style to decorate the weddings of Donald Trump,
Liza Minnelli, Joan Rivers, and countless others. He is the
author of* Preston Bailey's Design for Entertaining *and*
Preston Bailey's Fantasy Weddings.

In the 1970s I walked in to the home of two interior designers
and I was captivated by an explosion of beautiful gladiolus in a
glass vase. This one arrangement started the journey: my love of
flowers. Since then I have always made an effort to have flowers
in my home and in doing so have learned the dos and don'ts.
Here I will share them with you.

PLACEMENT

The most important way to give off a feeling of what your home
is about is to have welcoming flowers in the entrance. These
could be a beautiful blossom or a cluster of flowers. Each room
in the home should make a flower statement. In a contemporary
environment it is desirable to use the same kind of flowers. In a

more traditional setting, you might mix a variety of flowers and play up colors from the environment.

As you walk into your living room it is good to have flowers to help create intimacy, like on a coffee table or in a sitting area. When placing an arrangement on a coffee table, make sure it is not too overpowering and that it isn't so high that it prevents you from seeing across the sofa.

There are two rooms in which scented flowers are ideal. One is the bathroom and the other is your bedroom, beside your bed as you sleep at night, so that the first thing you smell when you awake is the wonderful scent of the flowers.

The rule of thumb for choosing a vase is that the flowers should account for 60 percent of the height of the arrangement and the vase should account for 40 percent.

LONGEVITY

Some flowers last longer than others. Lilies and any kind of roses, once treated properly, have long lives. Spring flowers, which include any blossoms, dogwoods, and lilacs, are tricky as house flowers.

To maximize the life of your flowers:

1. *Always make sure to buy freshly cut flowers.* Most flowers only last 3 or 4 days after they bloom so buying fresh is important for the longevity of the flowers.
2. *Maximize water intake.* If you plan to venture into blossoms, I strongly recommend smashing the bottom of the branches with a hammer at the base to aid water absorption. When removing thorns from roses, make an angle cut to allow the rose to drink water.
3. *Change the water daily.* When there is an arrangement in water, leaves should never touch the water—they will give the water a bad smell.

4. *Keep the water at room temperature.* The cooler the temperature in the room surrounding the flowers, the longer they will last.

5. *Avoid direct sunlight.* Most cut flowers need no sunlight.

FLOWERING PLANTS

One of my favorite ways to keep flowers in my house cost-effectively is to buy flowering plants. They typically last 1–3 weeks and the beauty is that if you get them in bulb form, you can watch them bloom and grow. Many bulbs don't need intense light, so indoor lighting is fine. Narcissus (paperwhites), amaryllis, and hyacinths make great home-flowering plants. Most flowering plants will require water daily or every other day. If the leaves start turning yellow, you are overwatering. If not, you are doing the right thing.

The best home investment is an orchid. Orchids are the most durable plants because they grow in extreme situations. If you hold on to the plant itself, it will bloom again. Some orchids bloom every 6 months, some every year.

SEASONS

Flowers are about life and joy. For maximum impact and beauty, pay attention to the seasonal ones. Here are some seasonal suggestions:

Winter: *amaryllis, poinsettias, narcissus, potted flowers*
Spring: *branches, daffodils, tulips, peonies*
Summer: *sunflowers, lilies, roses, stocks*
Fall: *hydrangeas (they dry beautifully)*

SENDING FLOWERS

When sending flowers to a home, think about the person and his or her style, and convey that to the florist. When in doubt, it is much better to send a simple arrangement and to always send flowers with the longest possible life. I recommend sending flowers half open, not yet bloomed, but not bulbs, so that the recipient gets an appreciation for their beauty upon receiving them. (When buying for yourself, you can buy completely tight bulbs.) It is always nicer to send flowers in a vase because the recipient can enjoy them right away rather than requiring them to perform work when the flowers arrive.

DECORATE WITH HOLIDAY LIGHTS

DAVID MURBACH

David Murbach has been manager of The Rockefeller Center gardens for twenty years. His most noted event is The Christmas Tree, which begins with the search for the perfect tree, the installation, and the oversight of its decoration with 30,000 lights. Murbach is credited with developing the techniques that ensure that the world's most famous tree glows from the inside out. He is the recipient of a Loeb Fellowship at Harvard's Graduate School of Design and a DuPont–Longwood Gardens Fellowship in public garden administration.

December in New York City is a magical time that starts with the lighting of Rockefeller Center's Christmas tree. The Tree Lighting Ceremony, watched by millions, is the spectacular climax to my yearlong search for the perfect tree and two weeks of careful attachment of 30,000 lights and a brilliant star.

When viewed from any angle, at street level or from the tallest building, the Rockefeller Center tree has an incandescence that radiates light from the inside out. Our "secret" recipe, which you can use at home by reducing the ingredients according to the size of your tree, starts with 5 miles of wire and 7A-sized bulbs (about the size of your thumb nail) at 12-inch intervals on the wire, in five colors. These "streamers" of wire and lights start at the top of the tree. The end of a streamer of lights is attached to the trunk, then tie-wired out along a branch until they reach the branch tip. The streamer is then brought back along the same branch to the trunk covering each branch with a pantheon of radiant, colorful lights. This process is repeated for every branch on the tree. Our streamers don't have plugs on the end like lights you buy for home. Instead, they have bare wire ends that are spliced directly into large power cables nestled against the trunk. This technique provides a safe, secure, and weatherproof system that artistically reinforces the three-dimensionality of this enormous tree.

To create the Rockefeller Center light effect on your home tree, follow these steps:

1. CHOOSE LIGHTS AND COLORS. Use your creativity to pick the appropriate lights and colors for your home tree. Lights come in a wide range of sizes, colors, bubble types, patterns, and multiple other options. I think simpler is better, so I recommend sticking with just one type of light throughout the tree. Test the lights at home before you put them on your tree. For safety, use a heavy-duty extension cord and a heavy-duty multiple outlet junction box to plug your light into. Also, turn off your lights when you leave the house and place a fire extinguisher close by the tree.

2. WORK FROM TOP TO BOTTOM. Always start attaching lights from the top of the tree and work your way down. With taller trees, you may find it helpful to put the lights on the top several feet while

the tree is lying on its side before you stand it up. Once the lighting is done, test it before adding any other decorative items like tinsel or ornaments.

3. CREATE A THREE-DIMENSIONAL LOOK. To achieve a three-dimensional look, you will need more lights than usual. Wrap the light streamers around each branch starting at the trunk. Then wrap them out to the tip of each branch and then back toward the trunk. Remember that you will need to plug the next light streamer into the last one and then plug into an electrical outlet. Plug nearby strands together and for those distant from one another, add extension cords to bring the plug ends down to a multiple electrical outlet at the base.

4. TRY THE ZIGZAG METHOD. A less complicated method is a style I call the zigzag method. From the top of the tree working downward, start your streamers with a light at the very top and zigzag from branch to branch, evenly spacing the lights throughout the tree, while working your way down and around the tree, getting some in the interior, some in the middle, and some on the branch ends.

5. CHECK FOR GAPS. Regardless of which method you use, after you have attached the lights, turn them on, step back, and look for gaps with no lights and reposition if necessary. If you used multicolored lights, you may wind up with clusters of one color so you can reposition some or switch individual bulbs to even out the mix.

6. AVOID THE WRAP AND THE STRIPE. There are two common methods of stringing lights that I suggest you avoid. One I call the Wrap, in which streamers are spiraled down the outside edge of the tree in a corkscrew-like pattern. The other method, the Stripe, entails running

streamers in rows from the top to the bottom following the surface of the tree. While these methods are fast and easy, they won't give any hint of the three-dimensional qualities of your tree. If you find yourself using the Wrap or the Stripe, maybe you should serve the eggnog after you finish instead of before you start.

TO RELATE

70

BALANCE WORK AND FAMILY

MARIE WILSON

Marie Wilson is founder and president of the White House Project, co-creator of Take Our Daughters to Work® Day, and former president of the Ms. Foundation for Women. She is the author of Closing the Leadership Gap: Why Women Can and Must Help Run the World.

Whether you have a family of ten or a family of two, achieving work/life balance can be extremely difficult, especially in this era of multiple jobs and minimal support. When we look into the eyes of our children and spouses, we often believe anything is possible—then we remember that we're not covered at work when our kids get sick or that we have no choice but to delay a long-planned vacation for a job crisis. Sometimes keeping balance feels like trying to empty the ocean with a teaspoon. To better balance:

First, ask for the help you need, whether it's childcare at home or in the office, flexible hours, job sharing, or family medical and paternity leave. This is easier said than done, of course, and it will require persistence and the help of other workers with similar issues. If you cannot get what you need at your current job, search for a company with good work/family policies, including one that understands elder care. There aren't many, but there are some. Naturally, if you can turn your company into one of them, all the better.

Second, many women and some men find themselves working a full shift (or more) at the office, then having to do the heavy lifting at home, too. It is important to understand and negotiate in advance. Sort out who does what from week to week, whether it's household chores or who picks up a sick child from school (and have a backup for times when neither of you can do it). If you haven't already made the choice, choose a life partner carefully—someone who has the same commitment to a balanced life as you and who is willing to help make it a reality. A special message to mothers: much is expected of you, and no one will have a higher expectation of you than you do of yourself. You will feel awful—like a bad mom—in those times when you choose work over family, even when you really have no choice. I advise you to ditch the guilt. It only slows you down. If you need a template for how to do it, watch most men.

Third, if you have children, remember that nothing helps with the strain like a "village" of help. "Other" mothers and fathers to your kids not only ease a very full life but can also bring richness to your sons and daughters. This is absolutely critical for single parents and for those who have more children than adults in the house (which is the point at which chaos usually reigns).

Fourth, understand that you will never achieve perfect balance. And that balance is different for everyone. It may be a spotless house to one person and basic hygiene to another. The important point is to *try*. It will keep you sane.

Fifth, make sure your children and spouse pitch in. This is not just about helping you—it's about transferring skills to the kids that they'll ultimately need. After all, they mess up their bedroom, they soil their cloths, they eat. They can help with the creation of order in the chaos.

Sixth, do some reading so you know you're not alone. There are many good books and magazines that offer everything from specific tips to complete manuals on balancing work and family. Many have struggled and some have written; you might as well benefit from their wisdom.

Seventh, get active. I know, I know—who has time? But if you can, join or contribute to groups that are working to change these work/life balance issues.

Finally, no matter what you do, there will be moments of utter insanity. But in the end, if children and spouses know there's thought and goodwill behind the attempt (and if they're working at it, too), much less will be expected.

71

SHARE HOUSEWORK

JOSHUA COLEMAN

Dr. Joshua Coleman is the author of The Lazy Husband:
How to Get Men to Do More Parenting and Housework
and The Marriage Makeover: Finding Happiness in
Imperfect Harmony. *He is a psychologist in private
practice in San Francisco and Oakland, specializing in
couples, families, and parenting.*

The person who cares more about the house being clean has to take the lead on discussions about housework. That doesn't mean that one person has to do all of the housework. It means that as the one who cares more, you can't afford to wait until your partner develops your standards, because, in most homes, that will never happen. Bearing this in mind, here are some suggestions:

BE ASSERTIVE

It takes power and strength to get someone to do housework who doesn't want to do it. Many women feel guilty and back down as soon as their partners start to grumble. However, many men feel guilty because they know they're not pulling their weight. Let your partner know that this is important to you, and you expect him to do his share.

BE LOVING

If you communicate your request with a criticism—"You're such a slob" (or "flake," "loser," or "mess")—odds are that your partner is going to go passive-aggressive on you, rather than pick up a broom. You'll also get a better response if you state your requests when you're feeling close, not when you're furious.

BE SPECIFIC

"My spouse should just see what needs to be done and do it without my asking." Maybe he or she should, but that opinion won't get you very far. Be concrete and detailed in your requests: "How about if we have a rule that whoever cooks doesn't have to clean" or "How about if we alternate weeks on doing the laundry." If your partner hates laundry, be open to negotiating or trading, but be sure that the trade is sufficiently fair so you don't end up feeling resentful.

NEGOTIATE STANDARDS

Don't assume that your high standards are the right ones for both of you. Lose the self-righteousness and the moral outrage. Studies show that more housework gets performed when couples negotiate and compromise.

HAVE REGULAR MEETINGS

Have weekly or semiweekly meetings about who will do what around the house. This will keep things current and decrease the chance for anger to build. Meetings should be short and to the point, a maximum of 10 to 20 minutes. Keep the tone friendly and upbeat. Assume good intentions.

CATCH YOUR PARTNER DOING SOMETHING RIGHT

Be positive and offer praise when your partner does something that you want him or her to do. "I really appreciate that you emptied the trash without my reminding you. That meant a lot to me!" "Thanks for not arguing with me when I reminded you that it's your turn to clean the bathroom." Be sincere; don't condescend.

APPRECIATE YOUR PARTNER FOR WHO THEY ARE

We're all more motivated to please our partners when we feel appreciated for who we are. Therefore, if you're going to raise the topic of housework and your partner is a slob, start the discussion by telling him something that you like. For example, "I think you're great at fixing things, and I love how handy you are. I'm wondering if we could also brainstorm ways to share cleaning the kitchen and doing laundry."

PLAY HARDBALL

If your partner completely blows you off, no matter how reasonable or firm you've been, then you have to get tough. This means discontinuing activities that you know he'll do if you don't. For example, if you pay the bills and you know that he can't tolerate late charges, tell him that you're spending so much time on housework that you're giving up bill paying. Or don't fold your partner's laundry or provide other household services if he or she is not reciprocating in a reasonable way. Again, the tone should be affectionate, but firm. "I love you, you're a great person, but I'm not willing to do more than my fair share in this relationship. So, from now on . . ."

72

COMPROMISE

JOY BROWNE

Dr. Joy Browne is a psychologist and host of the nationally
syndicated daily radio program The Dr. Joy Browne Show.
She is the author of numerous books, including Dating
Disasters and How to Avoid Them.

Compromise is a learned and peculiarly human behavior; in the jungle, it's dog eat dog, eat or be eaten. Because we are social and verbal, human beings have learned compromise as a survival technique.

I'm a great fan of compromise because not only does it craft calm from fury, but because it often elicits a creative solution that would not have occurred to either party independently; it can often get us out of our own way or our own rut.

The most important thing to remember about compromise is that it is seldom done with strangers. With a stranger in whom we have no further interest, we can holler, cry, stamp our feet, shake fists, and otherwise act like a barbarian because we figure it's a one-shot deal. Compromise, on the other hand, is a product of the willingness to do business on an ongoing basis. Both parties have to feel that they gave up a bit to get a lot; if there is a shared future, everybody needs to walk away happy.

So while a compromise always occurs as a result of a disagreement, this willingness to negotiate requires trust, goodwill, a minimum of fear, self-confidence, and mutual respect. Respect offsets the temptation to cheat, cut corners, or promise what you can't or won't deliver.

Compromise arises out of the heat of bumping heads but morphs into the relative calm and safety of trust. It also requires a sense of confidence and self-possession. If you don't feel you can get what you want, you're going to be defensive and cranky. And you have to know going in what you want: what's essential and what's not, what can be jettisoned and what's crucial.

Now that I've convinced you that you want to be the Great Compromiser, how do you do it?

1. To start, we must offset our inherent tendency to be defensive, self-righteous, brittle, arrogant, or unsure.
2. Be motivated, flexible, knowledgeable, and friendly. Both parties need to be motivated to reach a mutually beneficial solution.
3. Don't read minds. Start out by asking what the other party would like to see happen. This technique works equally well whether the issue is choosing a restaurant for dinner, a salary increase, where to go on vacation, the make and model of a new car, or the appropriate discipline of a naughty child. The content of the compromise is irrelevant to the process.
4. Prioritize. If you both know what you want and what is less essential, flexibility is not a loss of face or power. Prioritizing your wishes allows both parties to give up something less crucial for something more important. Nothing makes us more flexible than

knowledge. Knowledge allows for alternatives, and having choices makes everybody feel less like a victim.

5. All of this means avoiding like the plague the following: belittling, swearing, the words *always* and *never,* hurt feelings, and insults.

The cool thing about compromise is that you can learn a different way of thinking, behaving, and being. And the only tuition is the willingness to give up something that is less important (like getting your own way) to feel connected and involved. Good feelings means that in addition to the specific outcome, the affection and respect for each party to the other adds the thick, gooey icing to the cake.

73

HAVE A SATISFYING SEX LIFE

IAN KERNER

Dr. Ian Kerner is a sex therapist in New York City and the best-selling author of She Comes First: The Thinking Man's Guide to Pleasuring a Woman, *among others.*

The World Health Organization estimates that 100 million acts of sex happen every day.

Did you get yours?

The truth is that the best sex we ever had is very often the best sex we *never* had. Because when it comes to communicating with an intimate partner—sharing fantasies, desires, likes, dislikes—breaking the ice is often like breaking an iceberg, and, well, we've all seen *Titanic.* Yet studies consistently reveal that those couples with the most satisfying sex lives are the ones who are also most comfortable talking about it. So get those tongues wagging. Hopefully in more ways than one, gentlemen, because when it comes to pleasuring a woman, the tongue is indeed mightier than the sword. The vast majority of nerve endings that contribute to the female orgasm are located on the surface of the vulva—from the tippy-top of her clitoral glands (the "love button," so to speak), down through the labia minora (her inner lips) to the perineum (the smooth expanse of skin between the base of the vagina and the anus)—and respond to stimulation rather than penetration. So think outside *her* box and turn foreplay into *coreplay.*

Get cliterate! Most guys know more about what's under the hood of a car than under the hood of a clitoris. But with more than eighteen parts, twice as many nerve endings as the penis, the enviable ability to produce multiple orgasms, and no known purpose other than plea-sure, is it any wonder that sex researchers Masters and Johnson declared the clitoris "a unique organ in the total of humanity"?

Okay, women, now it's your turn to get in on the action. First off, you need to unprotect his privates. Men's genitals grow outward, and, from an early age, guys intuitively protect the "family jewels." But, over time, this desire to protect the testicles manifests itself as a physical "pulling in" that extends to the entire pelvic area. (If you don't believe me, next time you're on a dance floor, take a look at the guys around you—they're all arms and legs, like they're doing the "Dance of the Missing Middle.") From a fear of having their testicles rough-housed to sensitivity around the perineum to a "nobody touches me down there" attitude about the butt and anus, the male experience of sex is one that's controlled, contained, and limited to the penis. So break down the barriers of protection in his pelvis to get beyond his penis and give him a full-body experience.

Then show him that nothing's inevitable. Although many guys take the "Superman approach" to sex—faster than a speeding bullet—male sexual response actually consists of four phases: excitement, plateau, orgasm, and the refractory period (the part where he rolls over and starts snoring). Most guys crash through to orgasm, missing out on all the pleasures of the earlier phases, particularly the plateau phase where he teeters close to the point of "ejaculatory inevitability." So slow it down and show him how to savor every step of the trip.

Finally, remember that our biggest sex organs truly are our brains. A great sex life begins and ends in the mind. Stimulate your imaginations, don't be afraid to talk dirty or share a fantasy, and remember that our sexuality doesn't exist in a vacuum: it's a barometer of how we live. From diet to exercise to stress management and erotic creativity, make sure to embrace a "sexually fit" lifestyle.

There may be a hundred million acts of sex happening out there, but no two are exactly the same, and in the end it's about quality, not quantity. Make every day a new day in your own personal sexual revolution.

74

MAKE A FAMILY BARBECUE

AL ROKER

Al Roker is a host of NBC's Today *and a barbecue aficionado.*

A nine-time Emmy-Award winner, he hosts specials on Food

Network and is author of four books, including the New York

Times *bestseller* Al Roker's Big Bad Book of Barbecue: 100

Easy Recipes for Backyard Barbecue.

When my father taught me to never to get into an argument about religion or politics, he forgot to mention barbecue. A man will probably change his mind about what church he will worship in or who he will vote for before he will switch sides on what is the best kind of barbecue.

You see, almost every region of the country has taken barbecue in one form or another and made it its own. The secret to the perfect barbecue might be the seasonings, the type of sauce, or lack thereof. It can even be the kind or cut of meat. And when it comes to barbecue sauce, the debate can last for hours. Family recipes are closely guarded secrets; generations are sworn to secrecy. That's the kind of fanaticism that barbecue sauce generates. Personally, I feel about barbecue sauce the same way I feel about steak sauce. If the meat is good quality and is prepared well, sauce just covers a good thing. It's like owning a Picasso and spray painting all over it. You can do it, but why?

To create the perfect family barbecue all you need to do is round up the troops and be sure they have a desire to eat some of the best-tasting, best-smelling food on the planet—and have plenty of time to do it.

Now, let's get one thing straight. When most of us tell friends or family, "C'mon over, we're gonna have a barbecue this weekend," technically, we're lyin' to them. What most of us do is grill. We slap meat on a hibachi, a kettle, or some other grilling apparatus and cook our food over a direct heat source. The cooking takes minutes rather than hours. And smoke is not integral to the cooking. That ain't barbecue.

The best part about barbecue is that it is slow-cooked. In these times of rushing and getting things done as quickly as possible, you can't rush great ribs. Cooked slowly with indirect heat, they take on the flavor of the wood or special wood chips that actually create the smoke. There are many varieties of wood chips available, ranging from hickory and mesquite to apple wood and everything in between, so experiment. What's the worst that can happen? You've gotta make another batch of ribs. Boo-hoo . . . pass me another Wet-Nap.

GET COOKING

First and foremost, to make a barbecue you need fire. I'm not gonna get into the ongoing debate over charcoal versus gas. Whatever floats your boat or cooks your meat. But lemme say this: I love the ritual of getting the fire going on a charcoal grill. And today, you can buy ready-made charcoal chimneys, eliminating the need for lighter fluid and the petroleum taste it gives your food.

While you can barbecue almost anything, when most people think of barbecue in this country, they think . . . pork! I'm gonna talk about pulled pork, which is made from pork butt; this is a perfect meal when you've got family and friends over because pork butt (also known as Boston Butt) is usually pretty big and fairly inexpensive. And anytime you can walk into your local grocery store and ask for "butt," it's the start of a good time. The best part is that you don't have to go to a fancy butcher shop to get it. I usually go into my local supermarket and ring the butcher bell. You obviously can tell . . . I'm a butt man.

It takes the better part of the day to barbecue a pork butt, so allow at least four to five hours and plan to be around or near your grill during that time. If I call the barbecue for noon, I usually start my pork butt at about 7 A.M., and I always have hot dogs and hamburgers at the ready so that family and friends won't starve with anticipation. These are the appetizers to get your family ready for the main event.

Don't bother with fancy rolls or bread. Cheap buns (there's that butt thing again) and squishy white bread are the order of the day. They soak up all the juice from the pulled pork and absorb the sauce. Prepare a variety of side dishes or have family and friends bring some along. This, my friends, is good eating!

My Pulled Pork Recipe
Makes 10 pulled pork sandwiches or 8 platter servings.

INGREDIENTS

5 pounds fresh (not smoked) pork butt, bone-in (look for the cut sold as Boston Butt)
5 cups BBQ sauce
About 4 cups wood chips
⅓ cup BBQ Rub

1. Place the pork butt, fat side up, in a disposable aluminum roasting pan and sprinkle the rub all over it, making sure all sides are coated. You can grill it immediately, or you can cover it with plastic wrap and refrigerate it for up to 24 hours. This is preferable; the flavors will have time to sink in.
2. Soak the wood chips (hickory, oak, or apple) for at least 30 minutes in cold water.
3. Prepare a charcoal fire or preheat a gas grill for indirect grilling over low heat.
4. Drain the wood chips and add 1 cup to the grill.
5. Put the pan on the grill, cover, and cook the pork, without turning, until the skin is crispy and an instant-read thermometer inserted in the thickest part of the meat reads 190° F. This will take 4 to 5 hours, depending on the heat of your grill.
6. Don't forget to add more wood chips—and, if using charcoal, more coals—as needed (check every hour or so). You should have enough soaked wood chips for about 4 hours of cooking time; if the pork takes longer, you will need to soak more chips.
7. Remove the pork from the grill and place it on a cutting board. Allow the pork to cool enough so that you can handle it. Pull it apart with your hands, discarding bits of fat and the bone, and place the shredded meat in a bowl. Chop the crispy skin and add it to the pulled pork. (Try not to eat it all!)
8. In a large saucepan, mix the pork with about 3 cups of BBQ sauce and warm slowly over medium heat until heated through. In a separate small saucepan, warm the remaining 2 cups of sauce.
9. Serve the pork as is, or on white bread or a roll, with the extra BBQ sauce on the side.

75

MAKE A SCRAPBOOK

LEEZA GIBBONS

*Leeza Gibbons is the host of the nationally syndicated radio
programs* Leeza at Night *and* Hollywood Confidential. *She
is the creator of LEGACIES, a line of scrapbook products,
author of* Scrapbooking Traditions *and founder of the
Leeza Gibbons Memory Foundation.*

Memories deserve to be captured, celebrated, and left behind
as a legacy. It was while watching my mother lose her memories
behind the veil of Alzheimer's disease that I became consumed
with the world of scrapbooking. You will be amazed at how this
hobby becomes addictive and soul-satisfying. Even the very first
step in creating a scrapbook—putting your pictures and words
on a page—elevates them to something to be cherished and
shared.

PICTURES . . . THE STAR OF YOUR PAGE

Look through your pictures and identify the story you want to
tell. Is it playfulness, bliss, turning points? "Firsts" are always
fantastic subjects—first love, first job, first bungee jump!

Understanding that emotion will help you decide on colors and embellishments (those little extras like buttons, ribbons, and beads) that add dimension to the page. From here, it's limitless creativity.

For now, let's say you're going to do a page on your first puppy, a black Lab. You have a picture of him sitting in the middle of the huge mess he made. He is *100 percent trouble,* and this picture shows it. (If you're looking for a title for your page, though, you don't need one—you've found it!) If you do decide to use titles, I recommend ready-made alphabet tiles or stickers, or even your own handwriting. Then set off your title with a special element or color to show it off. I also strongly suggest journaling, jotting down your thoughts and insights and incorporating them into the page.

PAPERS

Once you've picked your picture the next step is to choose paper colors to accent the photo of your black dog. Let's go with a solid red background paper. Other papers can also be incorporated to match or accent elements of your photos. His collar, for example, could serve as the inspiration for a secondary color like yellow. This secondary paper can be used to create photo mats, border strips, or shapes to be used as accents or embellishments. Scrapbooking albums and paper come in many sizes, though the industry standard is 12×12 inches or $8\frac{1}{2} \times 11$ inches. If you are just getting started, I suggest 12×12 inches for a bigger workspace.

Make sure your pages are made of a good-quality card stock and are pH neutral, buffered, and lignin-free. Papers are the foundation of creative pages, and those of us who are obsessed with memory keeping have hundreds of choices on hand at all times! You can find good-quality paper in single sheets or packets.

EMBELLISHMENTS, ADHESIVES, AND OTHER STUFF

You'll want to keep your paper colors in mind when choosing ribbons and other embellishments. Embellishments can be quotes, silk flowers, Popsicle sticks, beads, buttons, and bows, not necessarily store-bought, but whatever tickles your fancy.

Next are your adhesives. It's all gotta stick together. Even the experts usually use a repositionable adhesive on photos. Most beginners like a glue stick (which is permanent) and mounting dots—small, round dots of adhesive you can put almost anywhere. Both are super easy to work with. Whatever you do, resist the urge to whip out the Scotch tape!

Papers, pictures, and embellishments will all need a little trim from time to time. For cropping or cutting these items you may want a rotary trimmer with a built-in ruler. You may also use a cutting mat, straightedge, and a swivel knife. Regular scissors are just fine, too!

PUTTING IT ALL TOGETHER

Once you've put your first page together you'll need an album to put it in. Get a sturdy album that will allow you to expand the pages as you create. Page protectors (the clear "pockets") are essential! Select albums and page protectors that are polyvinyl chloride (PVC)-free, lignin-free, and acid-free.

Pictures, papers, embellishments and adhesives, a few cutting tools, and your imagination are all you need. Scrapbooking is all about *you* and telling your story in a form that reflects your style. Once you've found your visual voice, you're ready to have some fun, so get creative and get started!

76

CARE FOR AN ELDERLY RELATIVE

WILLIAM D. NOVELLI

William D. Novelli is CEO of AARP, a membership organization of over 35 million people age fifty and older.

There is no perfect handbook for caring for an elderly relative. There are too many variables, including family history and dynamics, the physical condition of the relative, the resources of time and money available to you, and many more. There are some general and useful principles about caring for an aging relative, but how these principles play out in practice will also vary. Most important, you must be adaptable, flexible, imaginative— and patient.

First, if the person you are caring for is your parent, that person will always be your parent. Even though you are providing assistance, respect that you are the adult child to your older parent. You have not switched roles. Instead, you find yourself at a place in life where it is your turn to give back some of what you were given earlier in life.

Second, remember that there is more than just one kind of care. We tend to think of care as help with the physical activities of daily life. This may be the primary reason you are caring for your parent, but your parent's emotions and psyche need care, as well. For example, your mother may accept that she needs your help getting dressed, but she does not want to feel like a burden. Assess the things she is capable of doing for herself and, especially, for the family, and encourage her to do them as a participant in family life. Talk to her about whatever interests both of you, not just her health or needs: she is still a whole person. Be on the lookout for signs of depression, not just for physical problems.

Third, privacy is important. The "in-law suite" is ideal for your dad, but a room of his own (with a bathroom) also ensures a sense of place and privacy. And his space should be filled with familiar furnishings that will offer comfort. Also, his place, whatever it may be, should be accessible without stairs, if possible.

Fourth, older people can learn things and don't need everything done for them. Your widowed mother-in-law may be physically frail and never have handled the family finances while her husband was alive. But, assuming no serious cognitive impairment, she can learn to balance her own checkbook. Show her how to do it and support her as she does.

Fifth, caring for someone is tiring. Be sure you find some way to get some rest—perhaps turning care over to a sibling, another relative, or a paid professional every now and then. You will need the break, and you will be able to continue to provide care with renewed energy.

Sixth, if you are working, be prepared for a balancing act between work demands and caregiving responsibilities. You may have to take leave occasionally or, if you can afford to, cease working entirely, depending on your relative's physical and mental condition.

Seventh, if your aunt is suffering noticeable cognitive impairment, your job will become more difficult and time-consuming; as her dementia worsens, you cannot leave her alone for lengthy periods, and her level of functioning will decline. At this time, you should consider having additional help, from other relatives or professionals, at least for part of the day. If you are working, this will be an absolute necessity.

These principles may guide you as a caregiver. They are not absolute. You will need to adapt them to your particular situation. But I hope they serve as a point of departure on how to proceed with a very difficult, but loving, task.

77

MAKE TIME FOR YOURSELF

Cheryl Richardson

Cheryl Richardson is a lifestyle coach and best-selling author
of four books, including Take Time for Your Life
and Life Makeovers. *She led the Lifestyle Makeover*
series on The Oprah Winfrey Show *and was the executive*
producer and host of The Life Makeover Project *on the Oxygen*
Network and two specials on PBS. She is a columnist for
Body and Soul *magazine.*

$\mathbf{D}$o you find yourself waiting until life slows down to schedule some "me" time? Do you feel resentful toward those who seem to get your time and attention first? Well, I've got news for you: the in-box of life never empties. If you keep putting the needs of others before your own, or if you keep waiting for all of life's tasks to be completed before you allow yourself to relax, you'll be waiting a very long time. Here's how to make time for you!

1. REVIEW YOUR SCHEDULE

How you spend your time can mean the difference between a mediocre life and a life that feels meaningful and deeply satisfying.

What does a typical week look like in your life? How many hours are spent caring for others? To get motivated, at the end of each day, review your schedule and estimate the number of hours spent caring for others. Put this number on the corresponding day in your calendar and at the end of the week, add up the hours. You might be surprised by what you see.

2. DETERMINE THE ACTIVITIES THAT NURTURE YOUR SOUL

If there were more hours in a day, how would you like to spend them? Make a list of activities that make you feel nurtured or energized, the longer the better!

3. MAKE A "SELF-CARE ABSOLUTE YES" LIST

The key to reclaiming control over your time has to do with remembering to make time for those things that matter most to your soul. Too often we get caught up in daily responsibilities and end up sleepwalking through life. It's not until we get sick that we stop to consider how much we need time for our own care. Once you've defined your self-care activities in step 2, you're ready to create a daily reminder. Review your list and choose your five favorite self-care actions. Write them on an index card and label it "My Self-Care Absolute Yes" list. Here's an example of what I mean:

1. Spend quiet time alone reading a favorite novel.
2. Go for a walk in nature to enjoy the beauty.
3. Spend quality time with my partner.
4. Visit with a good friend at least once a week.
5. Get a pedicure.

Whenever you start to feel overwhelmed, resentful, or stressed out, refer to this list and think about the last time you engaged in one of these activities. If the answer is more than one week ago, take one self-care action right away. Doing so will not only give you instant emotional and physical energy, it will inspire you to take more time for your life.

4. GET COMFORTABLE WITH GUILT

As you start to make time for yourself, it's inevitable that you'll come up against a little guilt (okay, maybe a lot!). If you start to feel guilty about making your time a top priority, take that as a sign that you're on the right track. Most people feel guilty when they make their needs a priority; however, this step is critical to your well-being *and* your relationships. When we do things for others out of guilt or obligation, we're not doing them out of love—the highest motivating force.

A high-quality life starts with a high-quality you. Making your self-care a top priority is not just a nice idea, it's a necessity. When in doubt, keep the following analogy in mind: when flying on an airplane, parents are always asked to put the oxygen mask on themselves first so they can then care for their child. When you put yourself first, you're better prepared to be there for others without resentment or anger—a win for everyone!

78

KEEP IN TOUCH WITH FRIENDS

SUE ELLEN COOPER

Sue Ellen Cooper, aka Exalted Queen Mother, is the founder of
The Red Hat Society, a society focused on fun and friendship for
women over age fifty boasting over a million members.
She is the author of The Red Hat Society: Fun and
Friendship After Fifty.

During the course of a lifetime, each of us interacts with thousands of people, but only a very small number of casual acquaintances ever bloom into deep friendships. Let's define a friend as someone with whom you connect on a deep level, someone you feel close to, perhaps as close as you do to some family members. These are the people you truly care about, and these people genuinely care about you, as well, adding support and meaning to your life. A precious few of our friendships become even more valuable over time, as there are few things more bonding than a shared history with another human being.

Because of the inestimable value of close friends, we instinctively feel the need to hold on to them. But acknowledging the importance of nurture to the survival of friendship doesn't necessarily translate into action. Does the following ring a bell? "It's great to hear from you! I have been meaning to call you, but my life is just so crazy these days!" It is easy to become caught up in those activities and projects that scream the loudest for attention and relegate the really important things (such as feeding our most significant relationships) to the back burner. While our friends may well understand how "crazy" and busy we are, the fact remains that untended friendships can wither, or even fade away entirely, leaving one's world a colder place.

It is worth putting some conscious thought into how best to sustain these valuable relationships. Beyond that, it is necessary to back up your understanding with deliberate action: set aside time to touch base with your friends on a regular basis. Put their names on your "To Do" list. Build them *into* your weekly To Do list. This doesn't necessarily mean setting aside huge blocks of time; it can be as simple as a quick phone call to say, "I'm thinking of you. How'd that job interview go?" or "I just had to tell you what happened to me yesterday!" Make it a point to stay on the same wavelength with your favorite people. Sharing our daily lives builds strong bonds. Of course it will also be important to spend larger amounts of time together as frequently as possible.

That, in a nutshell, is how to *literally* stay in touch with friends. But there is another element to friendship—staying in touch *emotionally*. Here are a few suggestions for how to do that:

* *Let your affection show.* Tell your friends how much you value their friendship. Demonstrate how much you care by remembering the daily details of their lives. If they have good news to share, rejoice with them. If they are having problems, ask them how you can best offer your support—and follow through.

* *Be reliable.* Don't make promises that you can't keep. Have you ever had the unfortunate experience of having a chair pulled out from under you just as you were preparing to sit down? Don't be a person who often causes others to feel let down or disappointed.
* *Demonstrate loyalty.* Make it readily apparent that you are in their corner. There is nothing more reassuring than the sensation that someone is standing solidly behind you. But be sure that the loyalty is deserved. Don't fall into the "my friend, right or wrong" category. If you see your friend making a serious mistake, point it out with honesty—and *lots* of love! Encourage each other to be the best that you can be.
* *Apologize if you need to.* Mean it.

One cannot keep a good friend without expending a certain amount of effort. Develop your friendship skills by *being* the friend that you want to have.

79

CREATE A SCAVENGER HUNT

Elise Doganieri and Bertram van Munster

Elise Doganieri and Bertram van Munster are the husband-and-wife partner team who created the Emmy-winning CBS reality series The Amazing Race.

1. *Participants.* Create a list of people you would like to take part in the scavenger hunt. They should have a good sense of adventure (or be in need of a bit of adventure!) and, even more important, a sense of humor. Choose from family members, friends, or both. It is usually more interesting to set up teams of two; this makes for fun interaction.
2. *Timing.* Set the date on a weekend. This will help you avoid conflicts with work or school.
3. *Invitations.* Tell everyone to wear comfortable clothing and shoes. If teams are going to be picking up items, you might want to suggest they bring a backpack.
4. *The start and the finish.* Invite your guests over to your house as the starting point, where you will give out the first clue. The finish line can be a park, the beach, or back to your house.

5. *Scale.* Should the hunt be contained in a smaller area, such as a park, or within a specific town or city limit? If you want to do something around town, specify in your clues that they correspond with different means of transportation at specific locations, such as ("Take the bus" or "Take a taxi"). Or do the entire route on bicycles. Whatever you choose, consider safety.

6. *Theme.* Choose a theme like a birthday, a holiday, memories, or songs. Then decide which locations you want your teams to visit along the route to the finish line.

7. *Clues.* Write several clues for each team to find at each location. If you are going with the birthday theme, the clue could be "Make your way to Crescent Drive and find the house with the number that matches the age of our honoree. There you will find your next clue." It is always fun, more mysterious, and more challenging to make the clues into a riddle. Sticking with the birthday theme, one clue could send participants to the local grocery store to pick up one item for the birthday party. There you will have placed a checklist of items in a designated area at the store, and when someone has picked up an item they cross it off the list, leaving items for the next team to find. As each team finds an item, there should be another clue waiting for them.

8. *Permission.* For any private location be it a store, a restaurant, or a home, speak to the owners to get permission to use their location before making it a clue on your hunt.

9. *Duration.* It is a good idea to test the route using the riddles. That way, you can estimate the time it will take to complete and prepare accordingly.

10. *Victory.* It is always fun to have a prize for the first team to finish the scavenger hunt. The prize could be a small gift, trophy,

framed picture, homemade CD, or anything else tied in to the theme. And, of course, once everyone has completed the scavenger hunt, you can all enjoy the party together.

Most important, the idea of a scavenger hunt is to bring out the child in all of us. Have fun, be creative, and enjoy the adventure.

80

SELECT AND USE A BIRD FEEDER

KENN KAUFMAN

Kenn Kaufman is the youngest person ever to win the Ludlow Griscom award, the highest honor among birders. He is a field editor for Audubon *and the author of a number of books, including* Kaufman Field Guide to Birds of North America.

Bird feeding. It's not just for the birds. Seriously, it's not. It's for us.

Wild birds are tough little characters. In general, they can get by without handouts from us. We put up bird feeders for our own pleasure, to attract birds closer so we can watch them.

If you're handy with tools, and bored, you can make your own bird feeders, but it's faster to buy them. Feeders are sold at hardware stores and garden supply stores, and you can find an even better variety at a wild bird specialty store. Before you shop, it's helpful to know the links among type of feeder, type of food, and type of bird you'll attract.

The easiest birds to attract are seed eaters like finches, doves, cardinals, and sparrows or omnivores like jays or chickadees.

You can scatter birdseed on the ground (wild birds eat off the ground all the time), but a feeder will bring them closer to your window. A simple open tray, with a roof to keep off the rain and snow, will suffice. More convenient is a feeder with a raised hopper or reservoir that dispenses seed a little at a time: fill up the hopper and you can ignore it for several days. A hollow tube with small perches, dispensing seeds only through tiny portals, will selectively attract small birds like goldfinches, siskins, and chickadees, discouraging big eaters like grackles and starlings.

Choice of seeds is just as critical as choice of feeders. Cheap grocery-store mixes of birdseed usually include "filler" grain not favored by most birds. Buy mixes designed by experts or buy seed types separately: sunflower seed in the shell for cardinals, grosbeaks, and chickadees; white proso millet for large finches, sparrows, and juncos; nyjer ("thistle") seed for goldfinches, siskins, and redpolls. A mesh bag filled with peanuts is an effective, if expensive, way to feed jays and other omnivores. For feeding doves, quail, and other big birds on the ground, cracked corn is a cheap alternative.

Most insect-eating birds won't come to seed feeders, but some (especially tree climbers like woodpeckers or nuthatches) will come to wire baskets filled with suet (beef fat). You might get suet from your grocer's meat department, but wild bird supply stores also carry suet cakes made up especially for the birds. Peanut butter mixed with cornmeal is a convenient substitute for suet.

Hummingbird feeders are in a class by themselves: clear plastic or glass reservoirs, with red plastic ports from which the hummers sip sugar water. Commercial nectar mixes are unnecessary, because it's easy to mix your own supply, 1 part sugar to 4 parts water. Innumerable styles of feeders are on the market. I choose mine on the basis of how easy they are to clean. Hummingbird feeders need to be cleaned out every few days, more often in hot weather, so the best are those that can be opened up completely.

Put your feeders where you can watch them from a convenient window, close to shrubbery or other cover, but not close enough to enable cats to ambush the birds. In some neighborhoods, metal baffles around the posts may be necessary to discourage squirrels from gobbling all the food. Keep a field guide near the window so you can put names on your visitors. You can keep feeders filled all year, but you won't stop birds from migrating. Soon you'll see seasonal patterns: some birds arriving for winter, others visiting in summer. You'll see flocks forming and disbanding, parent birds bringing their young. Keeping a log of feeder happenings can involve the whole family, a priceless opportunity to pry kids away from the TV or computer and get them to notice the real world.

81

MAKE A BIRTHDAY CAKE

COLETTE PETERS

Colette Peters is the author of five books, including Colette's
Birthday Cakes. *Colette's Cakes, her specialty cake-designing
business, is located in New York. She has designed the Christmas
decorations at the White House and the windows at Tiffany's.*

Making a birthday cake is a lovely gesture to show someone you
care. All it takes is a little time and a good layer cake and icing
recipe. You can always use a mix for the cake and a can of icing,
but it's even nicer and tastier if you make the cake and icing from
scratch. If you don't have a favorite recipe for a cake and icing, ask
a friend or relative for a good recipe that's been tried and tested
many times.

INGREDIENTS

Have a complete list when you go shopping so that you don't
have to run to the store in the middle of your cake project. Here
is what you will need:

1. Cake ingredients
2. Icing ingredients
3. Cake pans (generally two 8- or 9-inch rounds)

4. Rubber spatula
5. Offset metal spatula
6. Nonstick vegetable spray
7. Waxed or parchment paper
8. Mixing bowl and mixer
9. Long serrated knife
10. Decorative serving plate or cake stand (this could be part of their present)
11. Piping bags
12. Piping tips
13. Colorful candies
14. Candles

BAKING

Give yourself at least a day in advance to make the cake, so that it can chill completely before you decorate. Prepare the two pans by spraying them lightly with vegetable spray. Next, cut out circles of waxed paper or parchment paper, made by tracing the bottom of the pan, and place the paper in the bottom of each pan. This will make it easy to release the cakes from the pans when they have cooled.

When you have all of your ingredients assembled, mix the cakes according to the recipe and bake them until done. Keep the cakes in the pans until they are completely cool; then wrap them, still in the pans, in plastic wrap and place them in the refrigerator for at least 5 hours. In the meantime, make the icing.

MAKING IT SPECIAL

When the two cakes are totally cooled, follow these ten steps:

1. Run the offset spatula around the inside of the pans and turn the cakes upside-down onto a rack. They should come out easily.

2. Peel the paper off and turn the cakes upright.

3. Place cake 1 in the middle of the cake plate, using a dab of icing to hold it in place.

4. Slice cake 1 in half horizontally with the large knife and remove the top layer.

5. Spread some icing on the bottom layer of cake 1. Place the top layer of that cake on the icing.

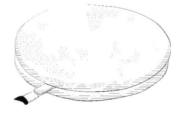

6. Cut the top of cake 1 so that it is flat, in case it has baked slightly domed.

7. Place some icing on the top of cake 1.

8. Cut cake 2 in half horizontally. Take the top layer of cake 2 and cut the dome off so it's flat. Place this layer on the top of cake 1.

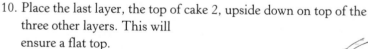

9. Spread icing on the top of what is now a three-layer cake.

10. Place the last layer, the top of cake 2, upside down on top of the three other layers. This will ensure a flat top.

Now you can begin to ice your newly four-layered cake. It works best if you chill the cake at this stage for about 30 minutes, to firm up the icing in between the layers.

Once chilled, spread a thin coat of icing all around the cake, using the offset spatula to get the surface as smooth as possible. Again, cool the newly iced cake. When finished, apply decorative candies and pipe icing around the base and anywhere else you wish. Try to be as creative as you can. Finally, place the candles on top, light them, and celebrate!

82

PLAY CHESS

Hikaru Nakamura

Hikaru Nakamura is the U.S. chess champion. In 2004, at
age fifteen, he broke Bobby Fischer's record to become the
youngest Grand Master ever.

Chess originated in India over 3,000 years ago. It is a fascinating board game that transcends language barriers and is enjoyed by people all over the world. While the number of possible moves in a game of chess can be mind-boggling, don't worry! It is easier to learn than you may think.

THE SETUP

All you need is a chessboard, pieces, and a partner. The chessboard consists of 64 light and dark squares equally divided among 8 rows. These rows in chess are called "ranks" and the columns are referred to as "files." The color of the squares alternates along ranks and files. The board is set up with a light square in the player's lower right-hand corner.

Each player has 16 light or dark pieces: 2 rooks, 2 knights, 2 bishops, a queen, a king, and 8 pawns. The pieces are arranged along the first two ranks for either side with the pieces occupying the first rank, and the pawns lined up in front. The rooks stand in the corners, followed by knights and bishops. The king and queen inhabit the two center squares, with the queen always placed on the square of her color.

THE MOVES

The *rook, bishop,* and *queen* may all move any number of squares without changing direction, as long as the coast is clear. The rook moves along ranks or files. The *bishop* may move only on diagonals. The *queen* may move in all directions. Of these pieces, the queen is the most powerful.

The *knight* is the only piece that can jump over other pieces. It jumps in an L shape, moving 2 squares along a rank or file and then 1 square to the right or left.

The *pawn* can move 1 or 2 squares forward from its starting square. After this, a pawn only moves 1 square ahead. Unlike other pieces, pawns may not move backward. If a pawn reaches the eighth rank, then it may be exchanged for any piece except a king.

Now we come to the *king,* the most important piece. The king moves 1 square at a time in any direction. The king must be protected at all times in order to keep the game going.

CAPTURING PIECES

Captures are made when a piece lands on the square that is being occupied by the opponent's piece. Pieces capture in the same way they move, with the exception of the pawn, which captures 1 square diagonally at all times. When a piece is captured, that ends the move. Any piece may capture any other piece, but nothing may capture the king, not even if a king were to walk into danger accidentally.

THE FINALE

A common misconception is that the object of the game is to *capture* the king. This is not true: the goal is to *trap* the king. If a king is attacked, it is in "check." A check can be parried in three ways: moving away, blocking, or capturing the attacker. If the king cannot escape check in any one of these ways, then it is in "checkmate." This is one way a game ends.

Another way a game ends is in a *stalemate* where neither player wins. This happens when a king is not in check and that player has no legal moves. A game may also end in a tie at any point by mutual agreement.

SPECIAL MOVES

Castling: The king and rook must still be on their original squares with no pieces in between. The king would move two squares sideways and the rook jumps over the king to the square next door. This moves your king out of the center of the board, which usually means it is in less danger of being attacked.

En passant: This is a capture only made by pawns. If your pawn makes its first move by moving 2 spaces forward and ends up next to your opponent's pawn, that pawn may capture your pawn by moving diagonally as if it were a normal capture. This must be done on the very next move or it cannot be played.

Chess is a game you can enjoy your whole life. It has taken me many places—from Iceland to Argentina, from Gibraltar to China. Who knows where you might find yourself playing your next game!

83

WIN AT POKER

MIKE CARO

Mike Caro, known as the "Mad Genius of Poker," is widely regarded as the world's foremost authority on poker strategy, psychology, and statistics. He is author of Caro's Book of Poker Tells, Caro's Fundamental Secrets of Winning Poker, *and other gambling and poker books. His research and teachings are credited in over fifty poker books other than his own. He is founder of Mike Caro University of Poker, Gambling, and Life Strategy.*

You've probably heard that you can't win gambling. That's silly—the money needs to end up in somebody's pocket. If you own a casino, then you're going to win, because the odds are in your favor. Poker, on the other hand, doesn't favor the casino—it is player against player, so you make your own odds. Eventually, the money flows from the bad players to the good ones. It's that simple.

You need to be better than your opponents to win at poker,

and here are twelve important considerations that can make that happen:

1. DON'T PLAY TOO MANY HANDS. A great portion of the profit you will make at poker comes from simply being more selective about the hands you play than your opponents are about the hands they play.

2. FOCUS ON MAKING GOOD DECISIONS, NOT ON MAKING POTS. Poker's biggest losers are the ones who win the most pots! Don't be one of them. Focus on making good decisions, especially if it means folding. In the long run, there's profit in throwing weak hands away!

3. LEARN THE BODY LANGUAGE OF POKER. Players' mannerisms, called tells, give away the secret strength of their hands. Most of your opponents fear they're going to accidentally reveal the true strength of their poker hands, pretending to be weak when they're strong and strong when they're weak. They're actors. When you see someone pretending to be weak—by shrugging, sighing, or betting in a sad voice—you should seriously consider throwing your hand away. That's a sign of strength. And when a player pretends to be strong, keep in mind that it's an act. You should often call that bet.

4. WATCH FOR INVOLUNTARY TELLS. One of the most important tells in this category is the suddenly shaking hand accompanying a bet. Most players instinctively misinterpret this as nervousness associated with a bluff. It is not! It is a release of tension that indicates the suspense is over and an opponent has made a big hand. Usually fold whenever you see a previously steady-handed opponent tremble while betting.

5. RECOGNIZE POKER BULLIES. These are the opponents who bet and raise so routinely it will make your head swim. Fight your natural

inclination to fight fire with fire. The way to destroy poker bullies is to simply call their bets more often and bet against them less often. Let them hang themselves.

6. CALL IN THE FINAL ROUNDS. On the very last betting rounds during a poker hand, it's tempting to make decisions about whether or not to call a bet based on your assessment of whether you have the bettor beat. That's the wrong way to decide. Usually, on the final betting round, the pot is many times as large as the amount it costs to call. That means you can profitably call, even if you're going to lose most of the time. You only need to have a hand good enough to win once in a while in similar situations to show an overall profit, realizing that just one win will pay for many losing calls. So, often call, even if you think you're probably going to lose this time.

7. AVOID BECOMING OVERWHELMED. Most beginning players are overwhelmed because there are many things happening simultaneously in a poker game. The trick is to focus on just one thing at a time. You'll be surprised how other important clues will appear automatically.

8. FOCUS ON THE GAME, NOT YOUR INVESTMENT. Often, I'll hear a player say something like, "I've got to call. I already have $250 invested in this pot." Yet all that matters is how big the pot is, how big your hand is, and what it's likely to cost you to proceed. What you have invested in a pot never matters at poker.

9. BEWARE THE "THRESHOLD OF MISERY." Let's suppose you enter a game believing that you could comfortably afford to lose $1,500 but not much more. You get caught up in the action and the cards are falling poorly. Before you know it, you're losing $2,000. But the agony doesn't stop there. You find yourself losing $2,500, $3,000,

and now $3,325. At this point, you've crossed the threshold of misery. You've maxed out your ability to feel additional pain. At times like this, players stop caring about making good decisions. Those decisions don't seem to matter to you at the time, but there will come a time when you'll wish you'd continued to make them. This is true in real life, too. When businesses or romances fail, you're apt to stop making quality decisions about other things. Always keep in mind that when you've crossed the threshold and maxed out your ability to feel pain, your decisions still matter.

10. AVOID *"FANCY PLAY"* SYNDROME. As you gain more skill at poker, it's natural to want to impress your opponents with your superiority. Many skillful players fall into the trap of trying to find the most unusual and potentially impressive ways to play hands, rather than the most straightforward and profitable ways. Unless there is a compelling reason to mix up your play, stick to the most obvious choice.

11. UNDERSTAND BLUFFERS. Bluffers don't move much and they often don't seem to breathe. They're afraid that anything they do might make you suspicious. When opponents have bet and are closely controlling their breathing, that's a time to consider calling.

12. PLAY YOUR BEST GAME ALL THE TIME. This is the long-term secret to poker success. It's easy to get caught up in the emotions and action that surround poker. No matter how many unlucky hands you've played in a row, don't self-destruct—leave that to your opponents.

Go win!

DISCIPLINE YOUR CHILDREN

HARVEY KARP

*Dr. Harvey Karp is an assistant professor of pediatrics at
UCLA School of Medicine with a private practice in Santa
Monica, California. He is author of two DVDs and two books,
including two best-sellers,* The Happiest Baby on the Block
and The Happiest Toddler on the Block.

L et me bring you in on a secret: the most successful parents
rarely need punishment to keep their kids cooperative. Sure, our
kids need us to take the reins when they push (or shatter) the limits, but to curb conflicts and boost cooperation, *prevention* is the
magic word.

Here are four simple tips to prevent meltdowns and help you
create the happiest family on *your* block!

1. WHEN YOUR CHILD STARTS GETTING UPSET, USE THE "FAST-FOOD"
   RULE. This silly-sounding rule is the best friend of skillful parents. Here's how it works: When you order a meal, the wait-
   ress never declares, "That's $4." Instead, she repeats your

order first. Only then does she take her turn (give her message) and tell you the amount you owe.

Similarly, in any conversation, whoever is most upset ("hungriest for attention") should have her feelings acknowledged first, before the other person gets to give his message of explanation or distraction. (Teaching kids right from wrong is much more successful when we shelve our lecture until after the hissy fit!)

2. WHEN YOUR CHILD IS EMOTIONAL, WHAT YOU SAY IS LESS IMPORTANT THAN THE WAY YOU SAY IT. Crabby kids pay more attention to our *nonverbal* messages (tone of voice, face, and body gestures) than to our words. So when your child is really upset, try the following techniques:

* *Use short phrases.* Long explanations sound like "blah, blah, blah" to the ears of a distraught child.
* *Use repetition.* Adults go blind with rage, but upset kids get *deaf*! Expect to repeat things numerous (3–10) times before your child even notices you.
* *Mirror the feeling.* Sincere gestures and tone of voice show upset kids we understand and care. Speaking too softly will make your child think you just don't "get it" and keep on yelling. If the crying continues after narrating back their feelings a few times, say something like, "Sweetheart, I know you're still angry, so go ahead and cry, and I'll check on you in just a minute." Turn away for 20 seconds—excessive attention may encourage the crying—then return and try mirroring his feelings again.

3. LOOK FOR WIN-WIN SOLUTIONS. Smart parents find compromises where both parties can feel respected. (Think of this as setting up detours instead of roadblocks.) Enforcing your authority will be easier when you relax expectations a little and look for "baby steps"

of cooperation you can praise and encourage rather than smacking down your child's desires with a flat "no." Fair compromises allow challenging children to be flexible, yet still save face. Be clear about the difference between emotions and actions. You may have to put the kibosh on unacceptable actions, but don't try to stymie your child's emotions. Unexpressed emotion can lead to stress as well as mental and physical disease.

4. KNOW YOUR CHILD! The best parents tailor their approach to match their child's traits. Shy kids, who feel overwhelmed by the unexpected, do best when forewarned about the day's plans. Spirited kids need schedules peppered with plenty of time to play. Savvy parents avoid meltdowns by sidestepping situations that they know are particularly tough for *their* kids—being overtired; overly hungry; cooped up; overstimulated by TV, sugar, or wild play; or surrounded by too many temptations.

DISCIPLINE SECRETS YOU WISH YOUR MOTHER TOLD YOU

A PARENT'S ROLE

It's hard being a kid in our world—overmanaged, overscheduled, overstimulated, and too little time to play. Sure you have to set consistent limits but at times, all kids resist, rebel, and talk back. It is just the nature of growing up. It is our job to set limits and guide our children down the path of life, but it is their job to push and test those limits. That is how they explore and define their world, especially toddlers and teens and children who are really spirited.

INSTILLING SELF-CONFIDENCE

A child's self-confidence needs nurturing every day. But you don't need to set off fireworks to celebrate every little triumph (exaggerated praise makes many children skeptical of your sincerity). The best way to build your child's self-confidence is to give generous sprinklings of respectful interest spread throughout the day.

Adversity from the outside world can make us stronger, but attacks from our family rot us away from the inside!

CRITICISM AND REWARDS

Criticism is fine—it's all in the way you do it. Always listen first before giving your message and make sure you criticize only the action, not the person. Your child is *always* a good person, even when he or she does totally unacceptable acts. Don't do things you will regret (spank, embarrass, demean, belittle). Children need to realize that even though they made mistakes, you have confidence that within their ability is the possibility to do better. Use small rewards. For preschoolers, I like stars; for school-age kids, try poker chips they can save and then cash in. Teens like to work toward a special privilege.

PROBLEM SOLVING

Listen with love, but don't fall into the trap of thinking you have to solve all your child's problems. Life is filled with rejections, bullies, and belittlers. And that's okay; we develop more character and personal strength from struggles than from our easy successes. Your calm attention implies that you have confidence in your child's ability to solve her own dilemmas. So listen first and don't rush your child past her feelings by trivializing the issue or "rescuing" her with your solutions. The struggle is how they learn.

Parenting is tough work, but nothing in the world is more rewarding. These years disappear faster than you can possibly imagine and never come back again. So stay patient and have fun! Treasure each day's little wonders.

85

FORGIVE

Frederic Luskin

*Dr. Frederic Luskin is director and co-founder of the
Stanford University Forgiveness Project. He is the
author of* Forgive for Good.

Learning to forgive can be a liberating experience. When practiced, it leads to increases in physical vitality and emotional well-being and decreases in anger, stress, and hurt. The ability to develop forgiveness proceeds through three stages. At the first stage you are filled with self-justified anger or self-pity. You have been hurt and you are angry at the person you feel wronged you. You blame the person committing the wrong for how you are feeling. It is their action, and not your choice of response, that you feel is the cause of your anger. You have forgotten that you have a choice as to how you will react, or you are so angry that you are convinced that it would not be right to forgive the offense.

The second step toward forgiveness emerges after feeling angry with someone for a while. You then realize that the anger does not feel good to you. It may be hurting your emotional balance or your physical health. Or you wish to repair the damage done to the relationship, so you try to forgive the person who hurt you. You may begin to see the problem from the other person's point of view, or you may simply decide to let the problem go.

The third stage comes after you have seen the beneficial results of forgiveness, and you choose to let go of your anger or self-pity more quickly. In this stage, the choice is to feel the pain for a short period of time and then work to either repair the relationship or to let go of seeing the situation as a problem. In either case, you decide to forgive because you see the benefit to your life. It is the practice of forgiveness for hurts small and large that is so beneficial to your physical and emotional well-being.

At the Stanford Forgiveness Project we developed the "nine steps to forgiveness" to help anyone move from the anger and hurt of disappointment to the well-being of forgiveness. These steps have been tested on people with hurts of widely varying degrees and have proven effective.

1. Know exactly how you feel about what happened and be able to articulate what about the situation is not okay. Then tell a couple of trusted people about your experience.
2. Make a commitment to yourself to do what is necessary to feel better. Forgiveness is for you. No one else even needs to know about your decision.
3. Forgiveness does not necessarily mean reconciliation with the person who upset you or condoning their action. You are seeking peace.
4. Get perspective. Recognize that your primary distress stems from the hurt feelings, thoughts, and physical upset you are suffering now, not what offended you or hurt you two minutes or ten years ago.
5. At the moment you feel upset, practice stress management

techniques such as slow deep breathing to soothe your body's flight-or-fight response.

6. Give up expecting things from other people, or your life, that they do not choose to give you. Remind yourself that you can hope for health, love, friendship, and prosperity and work hard to get them. However, you will suffer when you demand these things occur when you do not have the power to make them happen.

7. Put your energy into looking for another way to meet your positive goals than through the same experience that has hurt you. Seek out new ways to get what you want.

8. Remember that a life well lived is your best revenge. Instead of focusing on your wounded feelings, and thereby giving power to the person who caused you pain, learn to look for the love, beauty, and kindness around you.

9. Amend your grievance story to remind you of the heroic choice to forgive. Move from victim to hero in the story that you tell.

TO ENJOY

86

START A WINE CELLAR

Stephen Tanzer

Stephen Tanzer is the editor and publisher of the bimonthly
independent journal International Wine Cellar. *He has served*
as senior editor and wine columnist for Food & Wine *magazine*
and wine columnist for Forbes FYI. *He authored two editions of*
Food & Wine Magazine's Official Wine Guide.

Though virtually 99 percent of the world's bottles are meant to be consumed in the year or two after they are released, a tiny percentage of the greatest wines—most, but not all, of them red—do not reach full maturity for anywhere from a few years to a few decades after they have been bottled. By then you won't be able to find or afford them if they're not in your own cellar. Wines that are built to age are utterly transformed through a long snooze in a corked bottle: as a wine's tannins and acids gradually mellow, it takes on extraordinary scents, flavors, and textures barely hinted at in its youth.

The wines you carefully age yourself will not only be cheaper but will be far superior to most older bottles you are likely to find on retailers' shelves. All you need is a place that is dark, humid but not too damp (60–80 percent humidity will keep your corks moist—assuming you store your bottles on their sides, of course—without resulting in mold), odor- and vibration-free, reasonably cool, and safe from daily temperature fluctuations. A below-ground basement that experiences a slow, natural temperature swing from, say, 68 degrees Fahrenheit in the summer to 58 degrees Fahrenheit in the winter will do just fine. If you don't have a below-ground basement that stays cool during the summer months, you may want to consider renting space in a climate-controlled wine warehouse or purchasing a self-contained, refrigerated unit made specifically for storing wine (55 degrees Fahrenheit is ideal long-term storage temperature).

A few brief pointers before you start loading up your cellar:

1. Take a crash course covering the world's major wine regions before you embark on collecting or join a wine club that holds frequent tastings. By sampling recently released wines in the company of those more experienced, you can learn to distinguish between a wine best consumed in the near term and one that will repay aging.

2. Resist the tyranny of Bordeaux. Red Bordeaux has traditionally been the cornerstone of most great cellars—owing not only to its slow development and uncanny longevity but to its track record of price appreciation. But if you're cellaring wine to savor rather than resell, keep in mind that a serious Bordeaux needs at least a decade of aging before its tannins begin to subside, and a top example from a great vintage may require fifteen to twenty years to take on the velvety texture that connoisseurs prize. So you'll almost certainly want some reds that can be enjoyed earlier—for example, red Burgundy, Hermitage and Côte-Rôtie, Italy's Barolos and Barbarescos, and California's best Cabernets. The best of these can rival Bordeaux for flavor authority and complexity.

3. Don't overlook white wines, but be discriminating about those you lay down. Having become less carnivorous in recent years, the typical American wine lover probably opens no more than two bottles of red wine for every white. Still, I'd recommend a more conservative one-to-three ratio of whites to reds in your cellar. After all, it's always possible to find a first-rate, ready-to-drink, young white wine on the retail shelves. More important, relatively few white wines hold up, much less improve, with extended bottle aging. But dry Rieslings from Alsace and Austria and the somewhat sweeter examples from Germany can age magnificently, particularly in vintages with sound acidity. Aside from the greatest grand cru white Burgundies, I'd want Riesling in my cellar.

4. Reserve a corner of your cellar for sweet and fortified wines. The best Sauternes and Barsacs, along with late-harvest wines from Germany, Alsace, and the Loire Valley, are ideal cellar candidates because they require a decade or two of aging to express their extraordinary aromatic complexity and tend to disappear early from retail shops. And no serious cellar is complete without at least a few bottles of vintage Port. These special-occasion fortified wines can take up to twenty-five years to reach a mellow maturity and last for generations.

5. Finally, get your wines off the retailer's shelves and into your cool cellar as soon as possible. The objective is not to buy wine that's old before its time but rather to buy young wines and age gracefully with your bottles.

87

HOST A DINNER PARTY

INA GARTEN

Ina Garten is the author of the best-selling Barefoot Contessa *cookbooks and the star of her own cooking series on Food Network. She started her career in food as the owner of the famous Barefoot Contessa specialty-food store in East Hampton, New York.*

From the time I was married in 1968, I loved planning parties, cooking, and getting together with my friends. As time went on I learned what worked and what didn't. I learned that small parties were more satisfying than large ones and that Sunday lunch was a better time to invite guests than Saturday night dinner because people are more relaxed and the food is *so* much easier to make. I learned that entertaining is not about the food; it's about the friends.

How you invite people sets the tone of the party, so be specific. "Please join us for dinner at 7:30 P.M. to celebrate Phoebe's new book." "Skating and dinner at Wollman Rink from 6 to 9 P.M." A cocktail party usually has a definite time span (from 5 to 7 P.M.), while a dinner party is open-ended ("Come at 8 P.M."). The invitation tells the story. I like to let people know how to dress by telling them where the party will be held. A clambake on the beach encourages casual attire, while a garden party might suggest big hats and pretty sundresses.

Next, plan the menu. Good food is about making people feel comfortable. When deciding what to serve, first consider the time of day and the season. No one wants to eat a spicy chicken chili and hot apple crisp on a steamy summer afternoon, but it would be delicious on a snowy winter night.

Third, try to cook two things and assemble the rest. If I have my heart set on making roast loin of pork with sautéed cabbage, I might decide to serve ripe pears, Stilton blue cheese, and a glass of Port for dessert. It's easy to make and you won't spend the whole day on dessert.

Fourth, make an exact schedule: at 7 P.M. marinate the loin of pork and turn the oven to 425 degrees Fahrenheit; at 7:30 P.M. put the pork in the oven and shred the cabbage; at 8 P.M. take the pork out of the oven and cover with foil to rest for 20 minutes, and then sauté the cabbage; at 8:20 P.M. serve dinner. With a schedule in hand I'm totally relaxed, and I can concentrate on having fun rather than obsessing about when to take the meat out of the oven.

The next detail is setting the table: round tables are better than rectangular ones, and I like to choose a table that's a little too small for the group I've invited. If everyone's seated elbow to elbow, the party's more intimate and more fun. The right seating plan can also make a good party better: I put the most outgoing talkers on opposite sides of a round table or facing each other in the middle of a rectangular table. That way, we're all involved in one conversation, and it keeps the party from fracturing into separate groups: we've all been to a party where one group had more fun than the other!

Finally, I try to serve dinner at my table in the kitchen whenever possible. Not only do my guests feel like family, but I never have to leave the party to serve the next course. When someone offers to help with serving or the dishes, I always say "Yes"—it's not only easier for me, but it makes the guests feels like they're on the A team.

But remember the most important thing: your guests really want to believe that you whipped this dinner up in the ten minutes before they arrived. Make them feel welcome with good music, fun drinks, and lively conversation. And they'll all go home saying those magic words: *"That* was so much fun!"

88

CREATE A CENTERPIECE

DAVID TUTERA

David Tutera is host of Party Planner with David Tutera *on the Discovery Channel and the author of* The Party Planner. *He began his event planning business when he was nineteen years old.*

When setting your table for any occasion, always start with your centerpiece. It is the first thing your guests will notice upon entering your dining room and will be the primary visual statement at your table, other than the brief distraction of the courses being served—but remember, you eat with your eyes first! You should create anything that you can imagine with only one cardinal rule: make sure your guests can see across the table for conversation.

Here is an innovative way to create a centerpiece that you can translate into almost any party. It will make you look like a pro and you can simply add or change certain elements to adapt to appropriateness and time of year.

Start by deciding what type of party you would like to have. The time of day and who your guests will be will help determine the environment you will want to create. I suggest buying a few glass cylinders in various sizes and quantities, depending on the size and shape of your table. The great thing about simple glass vases is that they are inexpensive and versatile—great for indoor and outdoor use, floral arrangements, candles, water with floating candles, or even sand art.

Place 5 glass cylinders down the center of your table, with space in between (place the cylinders in a line, the tallest one in the center, then the shortest next, and the medium at the ends). It's important to keep the design symmetrical. Fill the tallest cylinder with flowering branches (such as cherry blossom in the spring/summer or pepper berry in the fall). Fill the shortest cylinders with river rock and a colored but unscented pillar candle. The two medium end cylinders can be filled with a monochromic nosegay of floral (any flower that is your favorite). If you're intimidated by floral, fill the two ends with water and color them with food coloring. Add a few floating candles and fully opened rose heads. Your tablescape can transport your guests to any environment—fill with sunflowers and grapes for a vineyard-style setting, or use sand and shell with sea grasses for a beach setting.

Like your home, your table should reflect your personality. Now that your centerpiece is created, here are some other table tips:

* Be sure to set your table in advance (but never preplate the food) and always use a cloth napkin accented with a simple napkin ring or a touch of floral.
* Use place cards, whether formal or casual; it shows your guests that you cared enough to think about where each person should sit for the evening.
* If you are entertaining a group of people who are not familiar with one another, have everyone switch places at dessert (you can put numbers or directions for guests to move on the back of their place cards).

A truly successful party will entice the five senses: sight, smell, taste, sound, and touch, so even if you are not a great cook, you can easily improve your party-throwing skills by making it look great.

89

PAIR WINE AND FOOD

ANDREA (IMMER) ROBINSON

Andrea (Immer) Robinson was named Best Sommelier in America. She is one of only nine women in the world to qualify as master sommelier. She is the author of Everyday Dining with Wine, *among other books.*

First, take heart: pairing is easier than you think! That's because most wines go just fine with most foods. Why? It's thanks to acidity—a component that launches the flavors of food. Think about Europe, where they enjoy wine with dinner (and lunch!) every day. In this case, folks drink the inexpensive local wine no matter what's on the menu, and anyone who's traveled there knows what a wonderful experience that can be. So if you've just grilled a steak and the rules say Cabernet but all you have is a bottle of Chardonnay, try it! If you like the dish and the wine on their own, you'll probably enjoy them together, too.

That said, putting a little bit of method into your matching will enhance even your everyday dining experiences exponentially. Start with the basic principles used by sommeliers—specifically, complement and contrast. Complement refers to similarities in the food and the wine that put them on a pairing par, and contrast means just that—dissimilar flavors in the food and wine that, because they're different, actually highlight and enhance each other.

Let's start with contrast, which is one of the most powerful concepts in food and wine matching because of what wine brings to the table—namely, the aforementioned acidity, fruitiness or herbaceousness (or both), and often spiciness, from the grape itself or from oak barrel aging. Each of these wine components acts like a spark plug, supercharging the flavors in food very much the way our favorite condiments do. For example, we use tart condiments to cut through fattiness, saltiness, or fishiness, like a squeeze of lemon on your oysters. In matching, sommeliers do the same thing with wine, pairing wines with vibrant acidity (sparkling wine, Pinot Grigio or Sauvignon Blanc for whites, Chianti or Pinot Noir for reds) with fatty dishes (think fried foods, cheesy dishes, and cream sauces), salty foods (such as cured meats), and fish.

The flavors of fruitiness or herbaceousness in wine create a wonderful contrast to savory/meaty flavors. So use the exotic fruit of a California Chardonnay or German Riesling, or the zingy herbaceousness of a New Zealand Sauvignon Blanc, to showcase Southwestern chili-rubbed chicken or ribs. The lush berry fruit of red Zinfandel or Cabernet Sauvignon can bring out the meaty richness of roasted pork, duck, or game better than any fruit-studded stuffing or sauce. And the spiciness of an Aussie Shiraz or an Italian Chianti will spotlight the savoriness in sausages, pizza, curries, and other spicy fare.

Now for the other side of the coin: a match based on complement works best in the context of body or, put another way, texture—light or heavy body, spare or decadent texture. This concept sheds light on the logic behind classic matches like a big red wine with steak (full body with full body) or Champagne with oysters (delicate with delicate). So think lighter grapes (Pinot Grigio, Riesling, Sauvignon Blanc, and Pinot Noir) with lighter dishes, and heavier grapes (Chardonnay, Merlot/Cabernet Sauvignon, Shiraz, and red Zinfandel) with full-bodied dishes.

Complement also works with flavor, though less often so. When the dominant flavors in the food are sweetness, tanginess, or earthiness, you can use complementary flavors in the wine to craft a winning pairing. The classic matches of Port with chocolate (sweet with sweet), goat cheese with Sauvignon Blanc (tangy with tangy), and Pinot Noir with mushrooms (earthy with earthy) put the pairing principle of complement to work.

90

MAKE HOLIDAY COOKIES

Thaddeus Dubois

Thaddeus Dubois is the executive pastry chef at the White House.

Creating these famous soft rolled-sugar cookies will be effortless but keeping them around won't be!

The Good Cookie Recipe

If possible, the recipe should be made one day in advance or at least several hours before rolling out. In addition to the ingredients, you will need a tabletop mixer or a handheld mixer with beaters, a couple of mixing bowls, measuring cups and spoons, rolling pin, cookie cutters, baking trays, piping bags and tips, parchment paper, scissors, mixing spoons, rubber spatulas, cups or small bowls, and airtight containers.

Makes 3–4 dozen 3-inch round cookies

¾ cup sugar
⅔ cup butter
⅔ cup shortening
orange peel, grated from ½ orange
lemon peel, grated from ½ lemon
1 large egg

1 teaspoon real vanilla extract
½ teaspoon salt
½ cup milk
1⅔ cup all-purpose flour
1⅔ cup cake flour
1 teaspoon baking powder

Preheat oven to 325–350 degrees Fahrenheit (depending on oven).

Combine sugar, butter, and shortening in a large mixing bowl and cream for 8 to 10 minutes using the paddle attachment or beaters until very light and fluffy. Add the grated citrus peels, egg, vanilla, and salt and blend. Add the milk and incorporate. The dough will be wet at this point.

In a separate large mixing bowl, combine the flours and baking powder and sift together. Add all of the dry ingredients at once to the dough and mix on low speed until incorporated. If using a handheld mixer, mix this part by hand using a rubber spatula or wooden spoon.

Remove finished cookie dough and place it on plastic wrap. Tightly wrap the dough and place it in the refrigerator for at least 3 hours or overnight.

To roll out the dough, lightly flour a cool work surface and knead the dough until somewhat pliable but not too soft. Roll dough to ¼-inch thickness using a bit more flour if necessary to prevent sticking. Use cookie cutters to cut out the cookies, keeping the space between the cookies very small. You can also use parchment paper to line the tray. Line cookies about 1 inch apart.

Bake until the cookies are barely light brown on the edges, 10–12 minutes. The longer the cookies are baked, the crunchier they will be. Remove cookies from oven, let cool slightly, and transfer to a cooling rack. To decorate, use Royal Icing or Decorator's Icing.

Royal Icing

Once dry, royal icing becomes shiny and hard. It can be made very liquid so that the surface of the cookie can be dipped, or harder so that the icing can be piped on the cookies for borders or other designs. Royal Icing colors well and, once dry, keeps the cookies looking good even if they are tossed around.

1 large egg white
1 cup (for soft icing) or 2 cups (for harder icing) powdered sugar, sifted first, then measured
½ teaspoon lemon juice

Place the egg white in a medium mixing bowl and, using the paddle or beaters, gradually add the powdered sugar until the icing reaches the consistency you want. Mix on medium speed for 1 to 2 minutes, adding the lemon juice. If the icing is too soft, add a couple of drops of cool water. If the icing is too thin, add additional sifted powdered sugar.

Decorator's Icing

This icing is for those who like soft icing. It will never get hard.

1 cup butter, softened
½ cup shortening
3 cups powdered sugar, sifted first, then measured
1 large egg white
lemon juice, from ½ lemon
½ teaspoon real vanilla extract

In a large bowl, combine the butter, shortening, and powdered sugar. Beat until light and fluffy using the paddle attachment or beaters. Add the egg white, lemon juice, and vanilla. Blend well.

DECORATING

Once the icings are made and the cookies are cool, you are ready to finish them off with rainbows of color, masterful decorating techniques, and endless creativity.

Liquid colors work best for coloring the icing. Once you have the icings made, divide them into small bowls or cups and color each one. Keep the icings covered once they are prepared, so they do not dry out before use. I recommend moistening a clean kitchen towel lightly and placing it over the bowls of icing and then covering it with plastic wrap. If well covered and refrigerated, the extra icing keeps about 1 month.

DECORATING TECHNIQUES

Dipping the entire surface of a cookie in a soft Royal Icing creates a flat, crisp, and glossy top. Piping soft Royal or Decorator's Icing helps to outline the cookies and add spurts of color. Use different pastry tips to create visual excitement. For a more homemade look, spread a medium-soft Royal or Decorator's Icing onto cookies. The effect of the icing can be enhanced by sprinkling jimmies or colored sugar over the icing while soft.

Once the cookies are completed, store them properly. The cookies with Royal Icing need to be sealed in an airtight container carefully stacked with parchment paper or plastic wrap in between the layers. Cookies covered with decorator's icing must be stored in single layers. These cookies will keep well for up to 2 to 3 weeks in a cool room (65–70 degrees Fahrenheit). Don't freeze the cookies once decorated because the icing tends to melt once defrosted. You can freeze the unbaked rolled cookies for up to 3 months. They can then be defrosted, baked, and decorated in a pinch.

So skip your local grocery store and head to your kitchen. You will be amazed at how fun it is to make one of America's most popular holiday cookies!

91

HANG A TIRE SWING

JOE L. FROST

Joe L. Frost, Parker Centennial Professor Emeritus, University of Texas at Austin, is a leading researcher on play environments and child development. He was president of the Association for Childhood Education International and president of the American Association for the Child's Right to Play. He is the author of more than a hundred articles and over fifteen university-level textbooks, including The Developmental Benefits of Playgrounds.

Playing with swings is a very valuable form of play, promoting social development, motor skills, balance, body awareness development, rhythmic movement, coordination, and strength. Swings are also props for dramatic or make-believe play, contributing to imaginative thought and problem solving.

To build a tire swing with scrap materials, select a well-worn automobile tire that has no exposed steel. Scrub the tire using dishwashing powder to remove road grime. The support for the tire swing can be an existing swing frame in good condition or a large tree branch. The horizontal support beam or tree branch should not be excessively high, and the vertical support beam or tree trunk should not be in the swing path while swinging.

Several types of tire swings are common. A simple design requires attaching a chain around the tire at one location and suspending it in a vertical position. The other end of the chain is attached to the horizontal support beam or tree branch. The chain should not circle the tree limb since this will eventually cause the limb to die. This single-person swing is the least expensive to make and is appropriate for children of all ages beginning at about age three.

12 – 18 inches

A second type of tire swing can be suspended horizontally with 3 evenly spaced chains attached to the top of the tire with U-bolts. The 3 chains are then connected to a tire swing swivel. Chains can easily be linked together with "quick links" available at hardware stores. This swing allows three children to swing at the same time, which facilitates social skills such as language, sharing, and negotiation.

Several other variations of tire swings are easy to make. A to-fro swing, allowing only back and forth motion, can be made by attaching 4 chains to the top of a tire (positioned horizontally), then attaching 2 of the chains to an overhead swivel and the other 2 chains to an additional overhead swivel. This type of swing, having little lateral motion, can be used in smaller spaces than the above types. All three types of tire swings offer similar motor benefits such as balance, strength, and rhythmic movement.

All rocks, concrete, landscaping timbers, and other hard materials should be removed from the area under and around the swing. Resilient material, such as river-washed sand or wood chips, should be installed under and around the swing and replenished as it wears away. The height of the overhead swing support and the distance of the swing seat from the ground should be adjusted to fit the age group of the users. The bottom of the tire swing should be 12–18 inches above the finished, properly maintained resilient surfacing, depending upon the age and size of child users. Adults should supervise children's play on swings.

A number of sources for tire-swing components—special tires, plastic padded chains, connectors, swivels—are available on the Internet. However, using all manufactured parts deprives children of learning to use tools, creating designs, and constructing from scrap materials.

Finally, swinging is fun! Adults should take reasonable precautions but then stand back and let children play.

Note: before beginning to build a tire swing, the builder should review the U.S. Consumer Product Safety Commission (CPSC) *Handbook for Public Playground Safety,* which is noncopyrighted and available on the internet at www.cpsc.gov.

92

DRAW A BATH

LAURA HITTLEMAN

Laura Hittleman is the corporate director of Beauty Services
at Canyon Ranch health resorts, with locations in Tucson,
Arizona, and Lenox, Massachusetts. She specializes in
developing spa and body treatments and educates others about
caring for and nurturing themselves through relaxation
and healthy beauty routines.

There's a big difference between taking a bath and drawing a bath. If you're going to bother getting in the bathtub, you might as well take full advantage of the chance to immerse yourself in a full-out pamper fest. *Draw* yourself a bath and enjoy this relaxing ritual with its tremendous healing and therapeutic benefits. Consider using the following bathing accessories:

Luxurious bath oils, bath bubbles, or sea salts
Netted sponge (not a loofah, which is too abrasive)
Pumice stone or pedicure file
Exfoliating body gel or cream
Hydrating shower gel

Cuticle cream
Bath pillow
Quality razor
Hydrating body lotion
Foot cream
Soft music
Scented candles

To create the perfect bath, follow these steps:

1. Draw the bath water to between 98 and 102 degrees Fahrenheit. If the water is too hot, it can make you feel lightheaded. If it's below your normal body temperature, you might feel cold and uncomfortable. For an energizing bath, keep the water just on the warmer side of hot. Add your oils, salts, or bath bubbles to the running water.

2. While you're waiting for the tub to fill, light candles, dim the lights, and turn on soft music—or keep the music off if you prefer quiet. For an energizing bath, keep the lights a little brighter.

3. Before you get in, exfoliate your skin with your body gel or cream. Rub a dab of the product—approximately the size of a quarter—in your palm to warm it up. Smooth it on from your feet up to your neck, in a gentle, circular motion to avoid skin irritation. Let the product do the work. People often forget their backs so you might ask someone to help you apply the product there, too. Rinse your hands when you're done and quickly smear the cuticle cream on your fingers and toes.

4. Get in the bath and enjoy how the warmth of the water makes you feel. The exfoliating product will melt off your skin. Try to keep

your hands out of the water while you're soaking so your nails don't become weak.

5. After about 5 to 8 minutes, use your pumice stone or pedicure file to smooth your feet. Gently buff away any rough areas. Steer clear of the smooth, soft areas of your foot. Don't try to remove any calluses; just smooth them over. Your body made the callus for protection and will make it again once you buff it off. When you're done, gently push back the cuticles on your fingers and toes with a damp washcloth.

6. For women, now it's time to shave. Gently use your netted sponge, saturated with the hydrating shower gel, to wash your skin before shaving your legs. You will have a beautiful, close shave because the hair is softened from the soaking.

7. You're almost done. Lightly towel off and slather the hydrating body lotion and foot cream onto your damp skin, a fitting end to your luxurious bathing ritual.

8. Your total bath time should be between 14 and 18 minutes. Staying in longer could cause the skin to dehydrate, defeating the purpose of a therapeutic, nourishing bath.

93

CARVE A PUMPKIN

AMY GOLDMAN

Amy Goldman is a gardener, seed saver, and well-known

advocate for heirloom fruits and vegetables. She is the author of

two books including The Compleat Squash: A Passionate

Grower's Guide to Pumpkins, Squashes, and Gourds.

There's something innately magical about a pumpkin lantern: it "bespooks" Halloween. Put jack-o'-lanterns on your doorsteps and on your gates as a powerful deterrent against evil spirits—and as an invitation to trick-or-treaters. Why use fireproof faux pumpkins or orange plastic leaf bags with ghoulish faces when learning how to carve a real live pumpkin is such a breeze?

Though pumpkins are members of the squash family, come in blue, green, white, brown, and stripes, and can have warts or prominent ribs, tradition dictates that we use the tall orange field pumpkins for carving. Their rinds are easy to pierce and their stems are sturdy.

TOOLS

In addition to a pumpkin in pristine condition, you will need pencil and paper, a Sheetrock saw (6 inches), a smaller saw

(2 inches) with saber-tooth blade and wooden grip, a long-handled ice-cream scoop, a butter curler, a paring knife, push pins, masking tape, and a votive candle with a candleholder. A pumpkin pattern book and pumpkin carving kit (with mini-tools) are optional.

METHODS

There are two basic approaches to pumpkin lantern design and both have their charms. The freeform approach calls for a design of your own making, whether it is drawn directly on the pumpkin or, far superior, drawn on a paper template. Nearly fail-safe for beginners, though less homespun and imaginative, the cookie-cutter approach employs prefab (and often fab) paper templates. Create or use a simple pattern with exaggerated facial features and a margin around the perimeter.

Find a sturdy work table (such as a butcher block) in your kitchen, gather your tools and a pumpkin, and garb yourself with an apron, smock, or old clothes; roll up your sleeves and remove your watch and rings before taking the plunge. It's best to stand while hollowing and cleaning the pumpkin. The pumpkin lantern needs a lid large enough in diameter to allow easy exit, so draw, as a guide, a free-hand ring around the stem in pencil.

To prevent your lid from imploding and extinguishing the flame, angle the blade of your saw inward at a 45-degree angle to the stem so you produce a lid that is supported by the pumpkin proper. Saber-tooth saws make the kindest cuts.

Set the lid aside and remove the seeds and stringy attachments with your hands, a knife, and an ice-cream scooper. The remains can be scraped out and the floor of the hollowed fruit leveled—for the candle—with a butter curler. (The nutritious seeds can be roasted and eaten or saved for planting.) If the paper pattern is too large or small, it can be reduced or enlarged on a photocopier. Affix the pattern to the pumpkin with masking tape, flattening wrinkles with your hand or cutting corners so the pattern conforms snugly.

Sitting down, place one hand on the pumpkin, and transfer the pattern by pinpricking deeply with a pushpin along the lines at one-eighth-inch or shorter intervals. Peel off the pattern. To avoid carving out the wrong areas, pencil in the lines and place an X on those spots that are slated to be removed. Carve along the dotted lines at a 90-degree angle, using a smaller saw to maneuver in tighter corners, taking care not to bend it,  and wiping away filings as you go. Push or pull cut pieces out gently; a knife can be used to pry them loose or slice them in two for easier removal. Your jack-o'-lantern will shine more brightly if you trim shadowy fleshy tissue inside the openings. Empty the shavings and situate the candle in its holder before lighting. Turn out the lights or wait until dark—it's showtime!

94

BAKE A PIE

Suzanne Conrad

*Suzanne Conrad won the $1 million grand prize at the Pillsbury
Bake-Off® Contest in 2004. She adapted a family-favorite
pecan pie recipe with refrigerated pie crusts and granola bars to
create her award-winning Oats 'n Honey Granola Pie.*

$\mathbf{P}$ie is a treat that every cook can create at home and there is
nothing quite like the smell of a pie baking in your own oven.
You simply need a classic recipe, a few shortcuts that don't sacrifice quality, and a bit of creativity to bake a delicious pie you'll
be proud to serve.

1. DECIDE ON ONE OF THE THREE CLASSICS: PUMPKIN, PECAN, OR
   APPLE. Search recipe websites, call a pie-baking relative, or
   dust off your tucked-away cookbook and find a basic recipe to
   use as your general guide.

2. RELY ON A FEW SHORTCUTS FOR SUCCESS. I choose to skip making my own crust from scratch and use refrigerated pie crusts
   instead. This allows me time to get ready and relax before
   guests arrive. Pumpkin pie, the darling of the Thanksgiving

table, is also an absolute cinch when you start with canned pumpkin and premixed pumpkin spice. If you can use a can opener, you can make pumpkin pie.

3. ADAPT THE RECIPE TO SUIT YOUR OWN TASTES. You can do this with just a few minor changes, but employ a careful hand with spices and flavorings so that the real essence of the recipe (whether it's the fruit or nuts) still shines. Here are some examples:

Make a classic pumpkin pie recipe all your own by experimenting with a new spice blend or adding an extra pinch of aromatic allspice, cloves, or nutmeg. Substitute 2 tablespoons maple syrup or molasses for the same amount of sugar or use a combination of white and brown sugar. With these twists, pumpkin pie is too tasty to make only for Thanksgiving.

Pecan pie is my little black dress of the pie category—elegant and easily dressed up or down. Keep it simple with a dollop of whipped cream. Dress it up with a splash of coffee liqueur or bourbon and ¼ cup dark chocolate chips added to the filling. Drizzle the finished pie with melted chocolate. Substitute real maple syrup in place of half the corn syrup, and add walnuts instead of pecans.

Admittedly, apple pie has been my nemesis, my Waterloo. I've found that the key to a great apple pie lies in the fruit. Depending on the apple variety, time of year, and the crop quality, you could get apple mush, lumps, or perfection. To overcome this, start with a basic recipe and experiment with various cooking apples available in your region. Remember that not all eating apples are good for baking. Don't be afraid to try canned apple pie filling that you can personalize with spice blends or a caramel drizzle.

Here are a few more tips for pie-baking success:

* Stick with a glass or ceramic pie plate.
* Use real butter and vanilla, fresh eggs, nuts, and spices for flavor and richness.
* Play with your pie crust for impressive presentation. Try different pie edges, adding tiny leaf or fruit cutouts along the edge with a little dab of water. Easier still, use a different tool to crimp instead of your fingers or a classic fork. Experiment with two of my favorites—a grapefruit spoon and a pickle fork.
* Think pie à la mode. If your creation gets a little too brown or crumbly, just remember that a scoop of vanilla ice cream covers a multitude of culinary sins.

Perhaps more important than tasting a delicious bite of just-baked pie, be sure to overindulge in the joy of sharing a warm slice with family and friends.

95

INTERPRET DREAMS

CHARLES MCPHEE

*Charles McPhee, aka the Dream Doctor, is host of the
nationally syndicated* Dream Doctor *radio show and author of
two books, including* Ask the Dream Doctor: An A to Z Guide
to Deciphering the Hidden Symbols of Your Dreams. *He is
the former coordinator of the sleep research laboratory at the
National Institute of Mental Health.*

Learning the language of dreams will forever change your
understanding of the world and of yourself. Research demon-
strates that children in Africa have the same dreams as children
in China, India, Australia, and the United States. People of every
country dream about being naked in public, about flying and
falling, about running from tidal waves (even if they've never
seen the ocean), and about being late for school or marrying faceless lovers. What's the explanation?

Beneath the fabulous diversity of languages, geographies, and
cultures that blanket the Earth—and that occasionally make us
feel separate and alienated from one another—the fabric of
human life is refreshingly universal. We all get embarrassed

(naked in public), soar on flights of confidence toward our goals (flying), have support yanked out from under us (falling), fret before overwhelming emotions (tidal waves), feel tested in our careers (back in school), and wonder about our true loves (marry faceless lovers). The bottom line is that human beings share much more in common with one another than they do differences, and our dreams prove it— every night.

BUT WHAT DID IT MEAN?

Dreams reflect thoughts, feelings, and awarenesses that were on your mind *at the time you had the dream.* When trying to figure out the cause of a recent dream, think about events and concerns that were occupying your mind the day before you had it.

LOCATION

If your dream is set at your office or in a business-like setting, know that it concerns issues related to your career. Battlefields relate to difficult periods in your life (struggles with finances, divorce, custody issues). The end of the world symbolizes anxiety about the future. If you're injured and recuperating in a hospital, know that you're nursing an emotional wound. Dreams that are set "back in time" (an earlier time period with different dress, for example) are not about past lives; they're about earlier times in your current life.

RECURRING DREAMS

If a dream is recurring, think back to when you first had it. Recurring dreams of fire in a family home, for example, that started at age seven, reflect feelings of crisis and emergency (fire) in your family life (family home) when you were seven years old. Likely causes include parental conflicts (fighting, separation, or divorce), a medical crisis, or a drug or alcohol problem that routinely threw the family into chaos.

If the dream repeats today, you'll note that you have it when current events remind you of the past: continuing dysfunctionality in the family, a new or ongoing medical problem, or a parent or partner who is still alcoholic or abusive.

FEELINGS

Feelings in dreams are never disguised, which means that how you feel in a dream is how you feel somewhere in your waking life. For example, a dream of fist-fighting with your mother-in-law doesn't mean that you really want to punch her. It *does* mean you are feeling frustrated with her, which is exactly how you felt in the dream—exasperated and angry! Similarly, sad dreams about the death of a child do not foretell the future. Instead, a parent is mourning the passing of a period in his or her child's life. It's a common dream when children first enter school (leaving a sad mom or dad at home) or when a working mom reenters the workforce after child delivery and is forced apart from her baby.

DEMYSTIFICATION

Be practical when thinking about your dreams. Beware crackpot theories, psychics, and other people without credentials or scientific research to demonstrate their claims. Your dreams do not come from another planet. They come from inside you, from your subconscious mind. You are smart and practical. So are your dreams.

96

BUILD A TREE HOUSE

PETE NELSON

Pete Nelson is the author of four books on tree houses, including Treehouses of the World. *He is a principal of the Seattle-based construction company Treehouse Workshop.*

Designing and building a tree house is as much fun as anything you can do. The key is to keep it simple. In the thirty-five years that I have been building tree houses, the only projects that lost their magic were the ones that bogged down in superfluous amenities like bathrooms with running water and full kitchens (although some of those were fun to build, too). All you need is a small space up in the arms of a tree that can serve as a place to inspire and revive the soul. The list of possible uses for a tree house is long, but the most important thing is to be in a tree. The transformative powers of a strong and vibrant tree should not be underestimated, and to be counted among those who recognize this fact is a good thing.

Designing and building a tree house naturally starts with the tree. Almost any mature tree will do, but in your search for the perfect tree-house host, look for signs of trouble in the canopy.

Are the leaves or needles dry or discolored? Are there excessive amounts of deadwood (which in many cases can be cleaned up by a good arborist)? Check the root flare. A healthy root system is the most important part of the tree, and if all is well, a tree will often have the look of a trumpet set upright on a table, resting on its flared bell. If using more than one tree, look for healthy trees that are spaced in the neighborhood of 12 feet apart. Also, think about how close the tree house should be from other amenities, such as bathrooms and power.

The most important part of the tree house itself is the platform. Throw out all preconceived notions of what your platform might look like and let the tree(s) dictate the structure of the design. A tree house needs room to move and flex, so the first thing to do is plan the location of the beams. I recommend building in the lower third of the tree and using beam spans of no more than 12 feet (typically 4 × 12s and sometimes larger). Start the design process by pinpointing the floor level in the tree (usually 8–10 feet for kids and no more than 18 feet for the fearless), and then take careful measurements and lay out a cross section on graph paper. The trees may offer an attractive starting point, such as a branch or crotch to set the first beam into. From there move around the structure and place beams in a way that the floor joists (usually 2 × 6s or 2 × 8s placed on end at 16-inch intervals) span no more than 8 feet. Our motto is "Perch, don't pin," so where a beam is needed but nothing is available to perch it on, install an artificial limb (basically, a huge bolt). It is important to keep penetrations in the tree to a minimum, so make each connection count. Also, posting down to the ground is perfectly okay in my book.

Now for the house itself. Building the walls and roof can be straightforward (imagine a small garden shed) or complicated (imagine the Taj Mahal)—it's up to you. The main thing is to build everything you possibly can on the ground. Just be sure to build the pieces in manageable sizes so they can be lifted to the platform and screwed into place. Frame and finish the roof in place, but be careful. Use safety lines and don't be stupid. Tree houses are the most fantastic of all structures, so be sure to build safely and with integrity so they will remain one of the best examples of who we are.

97

MAKE BREAD

MARYJANE BUTTERS

MaryJane Butters, wilderness ranger turned Idaho organic farmer, is the author of MaryJane's Ideabook, Cookbook, Lifebook: for the farmgirl in all of us. *She publishes the self-titled magazine* MaryJanesFarm *and created a chatroom called* The Farmgirl Connection.

Not so very long ago, bread was made using only two ingredients, flour and water. That was all—pulverized grains and good, fresh water. Naturally leavened bread, without chemical rising agents and baker's yeast (one variety of yeast singled out), is the authentic staple referred to as the "staff of life."

Baking bread using your own sourdough starter is better for you because the starter pulls in thousands of wild yeast spores familiar to your body from the air that surrounds you, rather than only one variety of yeast concocted in a factory. It's like the difference between the diversity of a rain forest and a tree farm. Fortunately, you don't need a brick oven like our forebears, but I do recommend flour milled from organic grains to re-create the delicious sourdough bread of our ancestors.

Sourdough Starter

2 cups flour
1½ cups purified water

Place flour and water in a clean glass jar or bowl and stir with a wooden spoon. Cover with a cloth and keep it on your kitchen counter. Each day, mix in an additional ¼ cup water and ⅓ cup flour. This needs to be done for 6 days. On the seventh day (it's downright biblical), the starter will be ready. It should have bubbles and smell pleasantly sour like stout beer.

KEEPING YOUR STARTER ALIVE

You must refresh your starter every 7 days. Remove 1 cup of the starter to use in a batch of bread or flapjacks; then replenish the remaining starter by adding ¼ cup water and ½ cup flour. Let it grow for at least 12 hours before you borrow from it again. If you can't use your starter every 7 days, get a friend hooked on sourdough by giving him or her a cup of your starter.

Sourdough Bread

1 cup sourdough starter
2 cups purified water
2 teaspoons sea salt
3 to 4 cups flour
1 tablespoon olive oil
1 medium egg yolk
1 tablespoon milk

Place starter, water, and sea salt in a large glass bowl and whisk for 1 minute. Stir in enough of the flour to make a firm dough. Turn onto a lightly floured surface and knead the dough for about 10 minutes, working in flour as necessary, until the dough is smooth and elastic. Shape into a ball and place in a large oiled bowl, turning dough once to coat the top with oil. Cover with a damp tea towel and let rise in a warm, draft-free place for 4 to 6 hours until doubled in bulk. Punch down and shape into 1 large round loaf or 2 baguettes. Place on a lightly oiled baking sheet, and cover again with a damp tea towel. Let rise again for 1 to 2 hours, or until nearly doubled in bulk. Place a shallow pan of water on the bottom rack of your oven. Preheat oven to 500°F. Make slits on the top of each loaf. Beat together the egg yolk and milk and brush on the tops. Place baking sheet on center rack of oven and bake for 15 minutes. Reduce heat to 450°F and bake for an additional 15 minutes, or until crust is a rich golden brown and loaf sounds hollow when tapped on the top.

And an added bonus of making the starter for bread is that you also have the ingredients for pancakes (flapjacks):

SOURDOUGH FLAPJACKS

1 cup sourdough starter
1 cup flour
½ cup purified water

Mix starter, flour, and water. Let stand overnight (about 12 hours), covered with a cloth in a warm place. Stir mixture well and carefully ladle onto a lightly greased griddle. Flip each flapjack after bubbles form and their tops have lost their sheen.

98

START A COLLECTION

HARRY L. RINKER

Harry L. Rinker is a principal in Rinker Enterprises, Inc., a consulting firm in the antiques and collectibles field, and the founder of the Institute for the Study of Antiques & Collectibles. He hosted HGTV's Collector Inspector *and now appears on Discovery Channel's* Pop Nation. *He is the author of numerous books including* How to Think Like a Collector. *His syndicated column,* Rinker on Collectibles, *appears in papers across the United States and Canada.*

I know something you don't know. There is a collecting gene in the DNA.

If the above is true, and I certainly believe it is, then the following is equally true: people who collect are normal, and people who do not collect are sick. Prove you are normal. Start a collection.

Here are ten tips for becoming a smart collector. There is no shortcut. Follow them all.

1. *Make collecting fun.* Collecting should never become work. If it does, walk away. Collecting creates a high that is far superior to that of alcohol, drugs, or smoking.
2. *Collect whatever you like.* Do not let others, not even Martha Stewart, tell you what to collect. Everything is collectible these days. There are no more closet collections. Most collectors begin by collecting something triggered by their favorite childhood memories. Go with it.
3. *It is no fun if you do not have money to spend.* Do not surf the Internet or attend an antiques and collectibles show unless you have money to spend. Collecting is about buying, never selling. Make certain what you spent is your disposable income. Get professional help if you are spending the mortgage and food money on your collection.
4. *Available display space needs to be considered.* Collectors receive little to no enjoyment from objects stored away. Keep your collection accessible. Fondling the goodies is one of the joys of collecting.
5. *Do your homework.* Start by visiting area antiques and collectibles flea markets, malls, shops, and shows. Surf the Internet. When you find a category you want to collect, focus on learning which objects are common and which are scarce. Pay attention to prices. Most objects you collect are mass-produced. If you commit to the hunt, you will find plenty of bargains. Buy reference books, but test the prices in them against those you find on the Internet. Price guide prices tend to be high.
6. *Understand what it costs you to collect.* What you pay for the object is only part of its cost. Factor in your time, shipping costs, and/or the cost of the hunt. Once you have done this, totally

99

PREPARE A TAILGATE

RACHAEL RAY

Rachael Ray is the host of 30 Minute Meals *and* Tasty
Travels, *both on Food Network. She is the author of a series of*
cookbooks, five of which are New York Times *best sellers,*
including 30-Minute Get Real Meals.

Tailgating is literally using your car as a party zone. It is driving
to a desirable location and pulling a party out of your trunk. I am
a big sports fan, so I love to tailgate.

I often find myself at sporting arenas in which I don't like the
food inside. If I'm going to a game at Yankee Stadium, I love a
ballpark dog, but they don't pack the right condiments, so I pack
a thermal bag with chopped onions, relish, and hot sauce. At the
very least, I always go to a game with a food strategy in mind.

If you are not a sports fan, these are great concepts to use
whether you are doing a block party, at a picnic at the beach, or
in your backyard.

LOAFING AROUND

My huge tailgate (or even potluck) favorite is the stuffed bread
sandwich and it is not even a recipe—it's a method! Start with a

ignore it. Who cares what collecting costs? If you want something and have the money, buy it.

7. *Buy objects for your collection, not as investments.* Antiques and collectibles are bad financial investments. You buy at retail and sell at wholesale. Antiques and collectibles are a great emotional investment. An investment in yourself!

8. *Create one collection you cannot keep a straight face when talking about it.* I collect airline sickness bags and toilet paper. Why toilet paper? All toilet paper is not created equal. I learned this when I was using the loo in the British Museum in London and noted that every piece of toilet paper was marked OFFICIAL GOVERNMENT PROPERTY.

9. *Use your things.* Everything that you collect was made to be used. It was not created to sit on a shelf or be housed in a cabinet.

10. *Collect for a lifetime.* I breathe. Therefore, I collect. Don't worry about the question, "What is going to happen to all your things when you die?" When you die, it is not your problem. I adhere to the concept that he who dies with the biggest pile wins. I have no objection to competition.

When people ask me about my collecting philosophy, I tell them I collect based on the "toilet principle"—every time I buy something I go into a bathroom and flush a toilet to remind me what I just did with my money. I was not put on this earth to make my children rich. Neither were you.

big round or long loaf of crusty bread (day-old bread is fine), thinly cut off the top, scoop out the guts, and fill it with everything you would put in an antipasto platter. For the bottom layer, make a relish either by grinding up pickled "giardiniera" veggie salad in the food processor or substituting tapenade, store-bought pesto, or ground-up roasted red peppers. For the next layer, stuff in whatever Italian meats and sliced cheeses you like. Then for the next layer, add Italian vegetables like canned, drained artichoke hearts, tender chopped sun-dried tomatoes, sliced marinated mushrooms, and pitted olives. On the top layer, put in mixed baby greens, torn fresh basil, and thinly sliced tomatoes. Then drizzle extra virgin olive oil, salt, and pepper on top and put the lid back on. Finally, wrap the entire loaf.

When serving, cut in wedges, like pie or thick slices, and by then all of the juices will have seeped into the bread to make a dripless sandwich, the best sandwich you ever had in your life. You can adapt it to anything. You could make it with coleslaw, Swiss cheese, and smoked turkey, or hollow out pumpernickel for a gigantic Reuben.

MACHO GAZPACHO

This dish is a must. Combine sweet canned tomatoes (preferably San Marzanos) in the food processor with coarsely chopped seedless cucumber, jalapeños or Serrano peppers, bell peppers (red or green), onion (red or white), salt, pepper, hot sauce to taste, and fresh cilantro. Grind them in the food processor in small batches, pour into a thermos, and chill. There is no set rule as to how thick or thin the gazpacho should be. I like mine a bit chunky with tons of extra hot sauce and black pepper. For a meal on its own, you can combine this with grilled shrimp made with lemon zest, juice, salt, and pepper. You can either dip the shrimp into the gazpacho as a shrimp cocktail or to be fancy, serve the shrimp hanging over your cup.

GRILL A GO GO

To build my Grill a Go Go, I nest two disposable turkey pans on the ground, fill them with charcoal and some wood chips, and put an oven rack on top—an instant outdoor disposable grill! I cook next to my car, and when I'm done I pour water on the grill to cool and chuck it.

I take a couple of pounds of chicken, meat, or fish and a half cup of chopped herbs to add to the meat once it is on the grill. I then fill a Ziploc bag with an acid, either balsamic vinegar or the juice of a couple of lemons, and some extra-virgin olive oil to marinate the fish or chicken. Montreal steak seasoning is my favorite for grilling. You can add it to the meat or fish when it hits the grill.

For veggies, you can slice them thin, add fresh herbs or extra-virgin olive oil and cracked garlic in a bag, and throw them right on the grill, too.

FINAL THOUGHTS

I like to round out the menu with olives, nuts, cheese, and fruits. You can buy lots of fancy food these days in a grocery store, from individual pâtés to a wide variety of specialty sausages and cheeses. Another thing I do is to buy a piece of Boursin cheese, unwrap it on a paper plate, pour tapenade or pesto over the top, and serve it with garlic or sesame flatbreads.

I always do store-bought biscotti or cookies for dessert. For adults, pack up wines and flavored coffee or make apple brandy with hot cider. For kids, make cocoa with a peppermint or cinnamon stick in a thermos; by the time you serve it, the flavor has permeated it to make mint cocoa or cinnamon cocoa.

I don't believe in drink coolers. They are heavy and they smell! Instead, buy drinks close to where you are going, picking up sodas or lemonade locally. Serious tailgaters invest in a portable table and a few fold-up chairs. You can pack everything in hot and cold bags (found in any grocer), and Ziploc bags are great for storing, marinating, and mixing!

It is always fun to entertain creatively in a parking lot. Have food! Will travel!

LEAD A HAPPY LIFE

Alexandra Stoddard

Alexandra Stoddard has written twenty-four books, starting
with Style for Living. *Her other books include* Choosing
Happiness, Things I Want My Daughters to Know,
and Living a Beautiful Life.

Happiness can be self-diagnosed. Whether you were born with
an extra happiness gene or you acquire happiness through nurturing your environment, you can increase your set point of happiness by 50 percent. Here's how:

1. LIVE IN THE MOMENT. Breath by breath, now is the only time to
   be happy. Happiness is an activity. Focus your energy on what
   is true and positive in all that you think, say, and do.

2. TAKE RESPONSIBILITY FOR YOUR PERSONAL HAPPINESS. Begin
   today to never blame anyone for your sadness. Take control by
   moving your energy toward those things you love, that make
   you feel happiest and most fulfilled. Don't make excuses. You
   can rise above whatever happens, even those things beyond
   your control. Outside circumstances should not define you.

3. VALUE YOUR LASTING HAPPINESS AS YOUR GREATEST ACCOMPLISHMENT. Happiness comes first—everything else follows. Ask yourself what will elevate your mood. It could be more sleep. Maybe you want to read more, take a class, or go on a spiritual retreat. Do what feels good. A happy life must include a careful balance between serving the needs of others and taking time to nurture your own mind, heart, body, and spirit. Commit to discovering the small steps that can change your life right now.

4. IDENTIFY WHAT YOU LOVE. Start by keeping a happiness notebook. Write down words that make you smile. Record what you enjoy doing, food you like to eat, your favorite music, colors, places to visit, people you love, writers and poets who inspire you. Collect pictures of objects you find beautiful whether they be gardens, animals, lakes, room interiors, or art. When you identify your preferences, your passions, and even your obsessions, you become more aware of the ingredients to your personal happiness. Incorporate more of them into your life every day.

5. BE INNER DIRECTED. What makes you happy could make someone else miserable. Don't look around at what others are thinking or doing to help yourself become happy. Draw a circle with a dot in the center. The center of the universe is the point where your consciousness exists. Don't let the whirling circumference of your life spin you around. Instead, act according to the wisdom of your heart. Stay calm, focused, peaceful, and happy in your own inner world. Nourish your soul and take time to enjoy what you do.

6. NEVER FEEL GUILTY. The more positive, enthusiastic, and joyful your spirit, the more power you'll have to make meaningful contributions to improve the lives of others. Guilt is easy to feel but use-

less and negative. Positive thinkers are clear thinkers. Be self-aware and accepting and look for happiness in the process of life; that is where you will find it.

7. CHOOSE HAPPINESS. Children are intuitively drawn to pleasure, and we should be, too. Choice by choice, step by step, you can walk toward a greater awareness of what truly creates your genuine happiness. By making a commitment to lead a happy life now, you will light your path. Enjoy the full range of your senses. Read great literature. Listen to inspiring music. Eat healthy food. Listen to the rhythms of your body. Choose your friends carefully. Look for the good. See and appreciate the beauty in nature. Always seek the sunlight.

The time and place to lead a happy life is now and here. Say yes to the invitation and you will be rewarded with personal transformation.

Live and love happy.

EXPERTS' WEBSITES

CREDITS

"Increase Your Energy" © 2005 by Jon Gordon • "Secure a Mortgage" © 2005 by Melissa Cohn • "Negotiate with a Contractor" © 2005 by Lou Manfredini • "Move into a New Home" © 2005 by Linda Rothschild • "Make a Budget" © 2005 by Lynnette Khalfani • "Make a House into Home" © 2005 by Sarah Susanka • "Create a Home Office" © 2005 by Lisa Kanarek • "Organize Your Finances" © 2005 by Dave Ramsey • "File Taxes" © 2005 by Bert Mitchell • "Meditate" © 2005 by Joel and Michelle Levey • "Grow a Vegetable Garden" © 2005 by Howard Garrett • "Build a Snowman" © 2005 by Jim Sysko • "Make Hot Chocolate" © 2005 by Maury Rubin • "Design a Family Room" © 2005 by Genevieve Gorder • "Make Spaghetti and Meatballs" © 2005 by Giada De Laurentiis • "Host a Houseguest" © 2005 by Patrick O'Connell • "Sharpen Knives" © 2005 by Daniel Boulud • "Carve a Turkey" © 2005 by Art Smith • "Have Patience" © 2005 by M. J. Ryan • "Secure Your Home "© 2005 by Al Corbi • "Prevent Identity Theft" © 2005 by Senator Dianne Feinstein • "Practice Home Fire Safety" © 2005 by Ryan Sutter • "Maintain a Healthy Refrigerator" © 2005 by Carolyn O'Neil • "Incorporate Fitness into Your Daily Life" © 2005 by Jorge Cruise • "Prevent Household Pests" © 2005 by Orkin, Inc. • "Dust" © 2005 by Heloise • "Reduce Indoor Air Pollution" © 2005 by Jeffrey Hollender • "Stock Your Medicine Cabinet" © 2005 by Isadore Rosenfeld • "Winterize Your Home" © 2005 by Danny Lipford • "Control Mold" © 2005 by Jeffrey May • "Care for Your Clothing" © 2005 by Steve Boorstein • "Protect Your Kids Online" © 2005 by Parry Aftab • "Plan for Retirement" © 2005 by Ric Edelman • "Clean Your Pool or Spa" © 2005 by Terry Tamminen • "Be Safe in the Sun" © 2005 by Fredric Brandt • "Make the Most of a Spare Room" © 2005 by Susie Coelho • "Organize Your Closet" © 2005 by Anthony Viderguaz • "Clean a Carpet" © 2005 by Carl F. Williams • "Unclog a Toilet" © 2005 by Raymond P. VinZant • "Fix a Faucet" © 2005 by Ed Del Grande • "Select and Clean Countertops" © 2005 by Terri McGraw • "Hang Shelves" © 2005 by Lynda Lyday • "Fold Fitted Sheets" © 2005 by Erik Demaine • "Control Clutter" © 2005 by Peter Walsh • "Do a Spring Cleaning "© 2005 by Tara Aronson • "Have a Tag Sale" © 2005 by Kristin Van Ogtrop • "Stock a Toolbox" © 2005 by Norma Vally • "Silence a Squeaky Floor" © 2005 by Tom Kraeutler • "Refinish a Basement" © 2005 by Kitty Barthelomew • "Install a Doggie Door" © 2005 by Ron Hazelton • "Keep Your Pet Clean" © 2005 by Charlotte Reed • "Clean Gutters" © 2005 by Michael Holigan • "Trim Hedges" © 2005 by Roger Cook "Keep a Home Smelling Fresh" © 2005 by Jo Malone • "Decorate a Bedroom" © 2005 by Celerie Kemble "Choose a Color" © 2005 by Christopher Lowell • "Paint a Living Room" © 2005 by Bonnie Rosser Krims "Light a Room" © 2005 by Debbie Travis • "Hang Wallpaper" © 2005 by Susan Sargent • "Select Window Treatments" © 2005 by Charles Randall • "Buy Art" © 2005 by Barbara Guggenheim • "Grow a Flower" © 2005 by Rebecca Kolls • "Design a Bathroom" © 2005 by Nancy Epstein • "Arrange Furniture" © 2005 by Nina Campbell • "Renovate a Kitchen" © 2005 by Fu Tung Cheng • "Stain Furniture" © 2005 by Steve Shanesy • "Clean Jewelry" © 2005 by Jacob Arabo • "Decorate with Flowers" © 2005 by Preston Bailey • "Hang Holiday Lights" © 2005 by David Murbach • "Balance Work and Family" © 2005 by Marie Wilson • "Share Housework" © 2005 by Joshua Coleman • "Compromise" © 2005 by Joy Browne • "Have a Satisfying Sex Life" © 2005 by Ian Kerner • "Create a Family Barbecue" © 2005 by Al Roker • "Make a Scrapbook" © 2005 by Leeza Gibbons • "Care for an Elderly Relative" © 2005 by William D. Novelli • "Make Time for Yourself" © 2005 by Cheryl Richardson • "Keep in Touch with Friends" © 2005 by Sue Ellen Cooper • "Create a Scavenger Hunt" © 2005 by Elise Doganieri and Bertram Van Munster • "Select and Use a Bird Feeder" © 2005 by Kenn Kaufman • "Make a Birthday Cake" © 2005 by Colette Peters • "Play Chess" © 2005 by Hikaru Nakamura • "Win at Poker" © 2005 by Mike Caro • "Discipline Your Children" © 2005 by Harvey Karp • "Forgive" © 2005 by Frederic Luskin • "Start a Wine Cellar" © 2005 by Stephen Tanzer • "Host a Dinner Party" © 2005 by Ina Garten • "Create a Centerpiece" © 2005 by David Tutera • "Pair Wine and Food" © 2005 by Andrea Immer Robinson • "Make Holiday Cookies" © 2005 by Thaddeus Dubois • "Hang a Tire Swing" © 2005 by Joe Frost • "Draw a Bath" © 2005 by Canyon Ramch • "Carve a Pumpkin" © 2005 by Amy Goldman • "Bake a Pie" © 2005 by General Mills • "Interpret Dreams" © 2005 by Charles McPhee • "Build a Tree House" © 2005 by Peter Nelson • "Make Bread" © 2005 by MaryJane Butters • "Start a Collection" © 2005 by Harry L. Rinker • "Prepare a Tailgate" © 2005 by Rachael Ray • "Lead a Happy Life" © 2005 by Alexandra Stoddard

ACKNOWLEDGMENTS

As with *100 Things*, *Life at Home* is the product of collaboration not only between the great experts who appear on its pages, but also of a remarkable team of professionals, a heartwarming group of enthusiasts, and an endlessly supportive network of friends and family. My gratitude extends to so many people who helped and continue to help make this book, and the Experts' Guide series, a terrific experience:

To the community of experts, now 202 strong, whose talent, delivery, and wisdom shape the Experts' Guides.

TO THE PROFESSIONAL TEAM:

Katie Karoussos for whom thank you is not possibly enough. Your commitment, creativity, and determination are—in every way—invaluable.

Jennifer Joel, a superior agent and friend.

The Clarkson Potter team, makers of the world's most beautiful books. There is so much that goes into the success of these books and you are there in every step.

Catherine Ross for being my favorite illustrator since age nine.

Tory Johnson for generously inviting me to tour with her last fall.

And for their counsel, advice, and encouragement along the way: Larry Kirshbaum, Tim Ettus, Rob Odell, Josh Lipschutz, and Rob Stein.

TO THE ENTHUSIASTS:

Countless people offered a slice of their energy and support to *100 Things*. There are some who contacted hundreds of people and special thanks go to Lenore Ades, Liz Biber, Kathy Blum, Jen Collins, Courtney Ettus, Holly Falk, Beth Ferguson, Amy Fierstein, Laura Flynn, Amanda Freeman, Jonathan Groberg, Lisa Jacobs, Eila Johnson, Richy Lee, Taran Lent, Michaela Leopold, Adam Nash, Erica Payne, Paula Pontes, Jessica Schell, Amy Slothower, Sarah Speer, Emily Stern, Adam Weene, Naomi Weinberg, Lucy Wohltman, and Bryn Zeckhauser.

AND TO MY HOME LIFE TEAM:

My parents for always prioritizing life at home above all else.

My precious friends for their loyalty, love, and for being there when it counts.

My entire family, near and far, new and old, for their tireless belief in me.

And most of all, to Mitch, my life partner, for insisting that I learn to enjoy and appreciate what life at home is all about.